“ Falling from grace, and raised up again ”

"FALLING FROM GRACE, RAISED UP AGAIN"

By: Charlaine Simpson

XULON PRESS

Xulon Press
2301 Lucien Way #415
Maitland, FL 32751
407.339.4217
www.xulonpress.com

Due to the changing nature of the Internet, if there are any web addresses, links, or URLs included in this manuscript, these may have been altered and may no longer be accessible. The views and opinions shared in this book belong solely to the author and do not necessarily reflect those of the publisher. The publisher therefore disclaims responsibility for the views or opinions expressed within the work.

Paperback ISBN-13: 978-1-6628-4591-8
Ebook ISBN-13: 978-1-6628-4593-2

First I have to say I never thought the day would come when I can finally get my book written, it has taken me a very long time. But through prayers and never giving up on my dreams, (I guess you would call it determination) and to never giving up on my faith.

I also have my children to thank, (Roxanne & Crystal) they have been my inspiration to keep going even when times get tough, They are my whole life, At times They where all I had to live for, Even though, I had asked Jesus into my heart I have to say I didn't fallow him, He never gave up on me, So I have to give credit where credit is due.. God will always be my God. I will for ever be in debt to my God. I will always have my children; and I wouldn't be here if I didn't have them they have helped me in so many ways, my mom for always believing in me, my grandma for always listening to me and never giving up on me (This book I dedicate to you Alma). My sister for being there when I needed a shoulder to cry on, and a ear to listen to all my problems, my brothers for being my rock. And last but certainty not least my Lord and savour Jesus Christ for believing in me when know one else did.

"My book is kinda like a diary I write in it every day or when I am going through some really ruff stuff. Each entry will begin with maybe a prayer or maybe just my entries of my diary".

Since I was a child I always wanted to write a book, but I never new anyone who could help me, so I thought to myself; I guess I will just tell my story. Now that I am older and wiser I can say I am very happy and pleased with myself for never ever giving up. "I am me and I can except myself fully"

The good we do is never lost, each kind act takes root and every bit of love we sow in time will bear its fruit. **Psalms 58-60**

God new in his great wisdom that He couldn't be everywhere so that's why He put his children in a loving mothers care!!

Dear Dairy; Wed, March 25th, 92

My morning prayer. Help me Lord to use this day wisely that there will be know sad regret. When evening comes for hours mis-spent, for work undone, let me not forget that things which seem important now to me might dwindle in the light of the eternity! So if I planned this day all wrong, please rearrange it lord and make it right, just let me glorify thy name, put first things first, I want thy smile tonight.

A Diary Entry:

Today I went into school late I had a good day I bought ken a new spring jacket, after school I went shopping for clothes and food. Cant wait to spring, I will be out of school. That's it Amen

---

Dear Diary; Thursday March 26th, 92

Today I went to school and I wasn't late, Mr Carny my math teacher. Today we had a police officer come in, it was good. Went to 241 pizza for lunch. We came home (my children and I) and had hot dogs for for dinner and french fries. I went to bed at 9pm.

Dear Diary; Friday, March 27th, 92

I went to school today I had an alright day I left around 1:15pm I was feeling tired. I came home went shopping for clothes and things, I got my check and I cant wait to move. Ken feels really upset about his life when he was a child he was abused. Emotions pour out and I understand him and wish I could heal the pain, the pain is to hard and to long for so many years of pain. He was abused as a child, he needs me and I am there for him. Sometimes I get upset when he is. I believe this is something that takes a long time to get over, the bad memories will always haunt him forever and I think that the worst is yet to come, for him. I feel his pain. Ron came today for the kids, I had know choice but to let them go. Life will get better that's what I look forward to. Thanks Amen

---

Dear Dairy; Saturday, March 28th, 92

My morning prayers.

Today I slept in till 10 am, then got up had breakfast and went out shopping again for clothes and food, I bought 2 tapes, Guns and roses, and Metallica, Exile light. I am very happy today, I cant wait to go out tonight and have some fun. Sometimes its so great to have a break from the kids.

Dear Diary; Tuesday April 1st, 92

Today I didn't go to school I was to tired to go, I had a pretty good day i cleaned the house and went shopping out to melvern town centre. Last night Ken bought me 2 night gowns and 2 pairs of underwear a top and a headphone set for my birthday all this early, before my birthday. I love him so much. That's it.

Dear Diary; Saturday April 5th, 92

Today I had a good day we went to morning side park, it was okay, a bit cool. Then we came home had lunch then off to the aquarium store to look at fish. My dad is great; he has let me drive the car every day except on cold days. I really do want to move because living in the basement has been a little hard, I have know bedroom and no kitchen and I have to use the bathroom on the main floor. I would stay but I need my own place.

Dear Dairy; Thursday April 16th, 92

My daughter Crystals birthday is today. Happy birthday Crystal. I went to school today, but the car didn't start because of the rain. There is heavy rain in affect in Toronto and surrounding areas. At school I couldn't help but get mad at Mr Wilson because he cheats at floor hockey (He's the gym teacher) and then tells other people that what their doing is wrong, when playing hockey. I told my friend Tina that she shouldn't be playing hockey when your pregnant and she got mad and went to the change room, when we where in the hallway I was thinking about her and I felt bad for what I said, then she yells back at me and says shut up Charlaine I tell her lets go out side and talk,I felt bad.

Dear Dairy; Friday April 17th, 92

Today is good Friday and sometimes I don't know why they call it that, I am very upset and frustrated because I am concerned about my family and my two kids, I don't want them to be hurt anymore they have been through so much already and I don't want anymore pain for them, they are already suffering because there father isn't in their life's and now they have to see Ken drinking all the time. I don't know what to do I am sick and tired of men around me that make my life miserable. I thought life was suppose to get better not worse. All I got to say is, I wont put up with being with someone who's making my life miserable. Please God help me to make my life better, and give my kids a better life that's all I ask for, for a better life.

Dear Diary; April 27th, 92

Today I feel really sad, my dad is gone, my parents split up and I don't know if hes coming back, my mother has gotten them in so much dept she spends to much money more then she makes. I don't blame it all on her, I know my dad has some part in this, but if she didn't spend so much and start bringing in more money then I know this wouldn't of happened. Sometimes I look back on my life and I don't know what I would do without my dad, now he might be gone for good. I do hope he will come around I love him so much. For my life it is so much better then 2 years ago, I don't know what i would do if I didn't have such a good mind to think about my life and the kids life's. Now that I am going to get married I do hope it works out, because I am not going to let things go wrong, not again. Ken is important to me. I hope I feel this way in 30 years from now.

Dear Dairy; Monday May 4th, 92

Today I didn't go to school, I had to stay home because someone was coming. I had a pretty good weekend. I got 2 seasons passes for Canada's wonderland for ken and I, we will go next weekend because the kids go to Ron's, that's if he picks them up this time. That's it for now.

Dear Dairy; Saturday May 16th, 92

Today we went to Canada's wonderland it was fun, but the bat ride broke down so we had to leave and go to another ride. The only thing I hate is it cost so much money because we have to pay for the food, we are not allowed to bring food in with us, other then that it is a lot of fun.

Dear Diary; Sunday May 17th, 92

Today we went again to Canada's wonderland, it was even more fun because we met some friends there, it rained but after all the rain we went on more rides then we watched the fire works, it was an amazing show.

Dear Diary; Friday May 29th, 92

I am going to school to drop off the check, then go to the bank, then off to the mall. We are now home and he has bought beer again, I don't mind when he buys the beer but I don't want him to get drunk again, I hate it when he gets drunk and starts on me for know reason. Anyway I am babysitting for my friend patty tonight, it's okay, her kids are not that bad after all. John is home now, I am going home to bed. Patty lives right across the street from me.

Dear Diary; Saturday May 30th, 92

I wish I hadn't made such a decision to let Ken move in with me, because he has brought so much pain and anger, and I already been through so much pain and resentful to Ron, and now I feel that I don't trust men any more. I don't need this in my life right now. Last night he beat me and throw me down the basement stairs and also throw Roxanne down and she landed on me, thank God she landed on me, then threw me off the chair and broke my chair and to top it off I was calling 911 and he tour the phone away from me and pulled it out of the wall, just so I couldn't call 911. Now I have bruises all over me, I don't want him here anymore. I want him to leave, and I will never put up with abuse again. He has put my kids and I in danger and I am like a mother Hen I protect my kids, as far as boyfriends go I don't need them, I have a enough of guys hurting me and treating me like shit, well not know more. God bless my kids. Amen

---

Dear Diary; June 3rd, 92

I had a very bad day today, I went to my friend patty's and we talked about things, and I said I am kicking Ken out because of the pain he has caused my family. He is a alcoholic, I lived with this before and I will NOT live with it anymore, and I know they don't change, they need help. Amen

---

Dear Diary; June 30th, 92

Sometimes I just hate Ken, yesterday when I went to him about being out for 8 hours and he didn't phone me, he said he asked God into his heart but some how I don't think he did, this is about the 18th time we have argued and I cant handle it anymore my life was happier when i was single, I wont give up on my kids I wont. They have been the centre of my life and will continue to be. I just pray and hope that there is a man out there for me, one that will respect me and treat me like a queen. I will continue to make a better life with my kids. I love them so much and I will change again for them. I will do this for my God and my kids, I have to believe life will get better. Love always and forever mom. Amen

---

Dear Diary; Tuesday June 30th, 92

Here I am sitting in McDonald's restaurant and I feel so alone and lost, I don't know what to do next. Oh Lord what is the next step I must take to make for my kids, I want them to have a better life then I did growing up. I have tried so hard to make my kids life's better, I don't know what next to do. My kids probably don't know how to love because all they see is fighting and malis, why is it that guys always try to change us in life. Why cant I just be me instead of always trying to be someone I am not. God you know how much I love my kids more then anyone else, please help me to make the right decisions and make their life better and happier please Lord. Lord help me see what I am doing wrong so I can change. Amen

---

Dear Diary; July 7th, 92

I am very happy now and I do think the Lord is with me every step of my journey, ever step I take He has helped me with so much. I am glad Ken is still with me and I am sorry for hurting him, he is sick and I have to understand that. We will get better together. He really is the best. I am really happy we are together. I know I have said some bad things about him but that was because i didn't Know him, so each new day I try to understand him better. Amen

---

Dear Diary; August 20th, 92

Today I am going into the hospital to fined out if I can have any more kids. I am kinda scared but it is only a minor surgery nothing really to worry about.

I hope everything goes well. That's it Amen

Dear Diary; August 21st, 92

Everything went good with the surgery,A little sore but I am good. And everything is going alright with Ken and I, I love him and I want the best for him I want this relationship to work and he believes in the Lord, we have had our ups and downs, but I think that is normal, life will get better I know cause we have God on our side. Amen.

Dear Diary; September 2nd, 92

We have some trouble lately and I really don't know how one person can take so much and not go crazy, I think I am a strong person at least I haven't went crazy, lol. I hope life gets better for Ken and my family because what would we do without my baby bonus. We would be out on our butts, This is one income I hope the government doesn't take away form us single mothers. Amen

---

Dear Diary; Monday October 19th, 92

I had a good day today I went to the mall(Scarborough town canter) then I came home did the laundry and cleaning my room, its been good lately we haven't argued in a long time, we went to Kens sisters house it was good. Life is good so far I just hope we don't ague anymore, I don't like the feelings it brings.

It was about 2 weeks ago when Graces sister pissed me off, I cant believe her she thinks she can have my man shes got another thing coming to her, I cant stand girls like her what a slut, I am glad we are having a good time together, its almost been a year now for Ken and I, cant wait till we get married, it will be great. Amen

---

Dear Diary; Tuesday October 27th, 92

Tonight I am home alone, I don't mind its just sometimes very boring, Ken went to bible study, he has changed so much I should give him more credit for all he has done in his life. He is a new man now and I am very pleased with his success, he has been going to AA and church, I am also very pleased with his attitude, he doesn't yell at me anymore. Its a miracle what AA and church can do for someone. God does work in the back round and I never want to loose hope again. Thank you God for everything you are doing in my life. Ken is so much better now and the more he gets better the more I love him, I do hope some day I can have a another baby, he would be so happy to have a baby from me. Thank you Lord for everything you have done for me. Amen

---

Dear Lord; Thursday October 29th, 92

It has come again where I have to ask please give me a sign to know if Ken is the one for me, and help me to know what is right, I plan to spend the rest of my life with Ken, Please let me know if this is the right man for me. I am really upset right today, somehow I cannot trust him at all now and I know it will be a while before I can trust him again. In these rough times I can make it through I am strong because you Lord help me to be strong, this time I am going to be wiser in my decisions, I have sinned I know, and if this is a lesson I must learn, I have complete understanding of why, God please be with me now. Amen

---

Dear Diary; Monday November 2nd, 02

Today it is raining and cold outside, I was going to go out but decided to stay in, I really don't want to go out in the rain. Yesterday was good I went to Crysta's baby shower (KEN SISTER)she got a lot of nice things for her and the baby. I hope she likes what I got her and the baby. Amen.

Dear Diary; November 24th, 92

Today I went to court and Ron was not there, I am trying to get full custody. It is raining outside and Ken is at work, he had someone hit him from behind in a car, and I hope nothing is wrong with him. Our relationship is good, Ken is recovering and becoming a new man, Considering how much he has been through in his life. I have faith in the Lord, He has made so many changes in my life and in kens too. Amen

---

Dear Dairy; Tuesday April 27th, 93

I had a good day today, Sometimes the kids get to me, I love them but they drive me crazy sometimes, I think I need some time away. I love my new life and I cant wait till the next day to see what it brings me. I cant wait till the kids are in school full days. Then I can start my new carrier I am not sure exactly what I want to do but I do have an idea in mind. I would love to work in an office just to see if I would like it or not. I am going to go to collage to see if I can get my degree in a office work. Then I can learn the computer skills to work in an office.

Now is the best time while I am still young and I will have a good job for when my kids are older and wiser. Then I can get what ever they need and want. Amen

---

Dear Diary; April 27th, 93

I am just sitting here thinking about my life and I was thinking wow I have really been through a lot good and bad and great times. I have lived through it and I am much stronger today then 4 years ago, I am not with Ken any more and I am very happy with the decision. Maybe 3 years ago I might of thought i couldn't make it, but that is how life is. I am starting a new life being single again. You have to take that first step forward to say yes I can do this. That's what I say now, "Yes I can do this".

My cat smoky had her kittens about three days ago, they are so cute. I went on the woman's weekend and I found myself again, I realize now it wasn't always the guys I was with, I had something to do with it to. I am me and I can except myself fully now. Amen

---

Dear Diary; Wednesday April 28th, 93

I feel okay today and the weather is pretty nice out, I am very proud to be a single mother, I am finding myself again and I am enjoying life again. I am having a lot of fun meeting new people and I am enjoying going out on weekends. This weekend Roxanne is going to camp, and I am going to have some alone time with Crystal this weekend. Amen

---

Dear Dairy; Monday May 2nd, 93

Today I am sending out my secret letter to Ron, just so he knows I just want to be friends. This is for the kids, so they feel loved by both parents. The weekend is over and I feel tired, I have a very good weekend with Crystal, we went to Hastings on Saturday morning and stayed over night Crystal had fun and so did I. I love Roxanne and Crystal. Amen

---

Dear Diary; May 5th, 93

Today I had a good day I cleaned up my home and then had a nap, Crystal and I played with the kittens. There is this guy I talk to to over the phone he seems okay, his parents drink a lot and I don't want to get caught up in that again so I will just be friends. I want to be sure who I spend my time with. I want to go back to school soon so I can support the kids and I. Amen

---

Dear Diary; Tuesday May 11th, 93

Today Crystal and I went down town to see Ron's house and from there we went to a park, it was okay Crystal and I had fun, it was a wonderful day the sun was shinning and it was hot. Even though Ron is the way he is, he still is their father and I think he has the right to see them. Amen

---

Dear Diary; Thursday May 13th, 93

Last night I went to another meeting and I felt OK the first hour and a half, but once we got into telling each other what we think of each other I started feeling like I was a child again, like I am immature and that really hurt me, because I thought I was growing up, considering how I was 4 years ago, if only they new how I was then, they would think I was immature then. Maybe I still need some growing up to do. I just wonder if I can go and be with them again seeing I am so immature. I wonder if their just acting like they like me and they really don't. Now I am wondering, I guess I will just show them how mature I am really am. That's what I will do. Amen

---

Dear Dairy; May 18th, 93

Today is an okay day, but I have a few things on my mind and I need to figure things out. 1. I want to go away on the may 24 weekend and I have a meeting on Monday but I don't think I will be back in time to get the kids then go out to Col-borne. I think I should just stay home and that way I can go to church and go to the meeting as well. I don't know if Ron is going to take the kids anyway. Amen

---

Dear Diary; May 22nd, 93

Today I am doing fine, last night I stayed up till 3:30 am it was fun Grace came over and we partied. We had a good time together. Tonight I am going to have a party I hope everyone shows up. Its a long weekend and I am not gone away, oh well I will make the best of it. And I have to work at church this weekend, and then I have a meeting at 2:30 pm on Monday. Amen

---

Dear Diary; Tuesday May 25th, 93

Today I went on my second date, but he is not the one, I guess I have to keep looking for me and the kids, I want a good man, all I ever wanted for the kids is a good man to be their daddy. I guess it will take a few men to meet the right one. At least I know I have the Lord and he will never let me down. Amen

---

Dear Diary; May 28th, 93

Today I went on another date, it was good I had Crystal with me and he seems like a nice guy and he is good looking to. His name is Mike, I am not sure if he likes me though, but you never know time will tell, it could turn out to be good and we will start dating. He is 29 years old and has his own career, that is great. Amen

---

Dear Diary; May 31st, 93

Today I went to the mall with Crystal and bought her an ice-cream and Nachos. I had an okay day I felt a little bit better today, it was nice out not to hot today,.

Oh Lord please forgive me what have I gotten myself into now and how do I make it right. Amen

---

Dear Diary; June 1st, 93

Today I went grocery shopping and I got back just in time to pick up Crystal from school. A lot of people from my team seem to be calling me more then ever before and it makes me wonder, (Do I sound like something is wrong with me) Can they really tell by the tone of my voice or do they know something is wrong with me? I don't know but I am okay, I will survive this I know I will. Amen

---

Dear Diary; June 6th, 93

Today I am regretful the kids are still with their dad, he took them on Friday and Friday I went to Etobicoke to see mike and Kelly both guys, we watched a movie then I went to bed in their guest room, (by myself I might add) So I feel whole lot better now that I've gotten some things off my mind I think it does me good when I have time away from the kids, I am so busy with them all the time. I can find myself again and get back on track. This is really great for the kids because then I can be a lot happier with them, we all benefit in the end. Thank you Lord for always looking out after us all. I love you Roxanne and Crystal. Love you to the moon and back, Thank you Jesus for working in the back round and never giving up on me. Amen

---

Dear Diary; June 11th, 93

Today I had a very good day, it was sunny out and hot, the kids are now out playing and they just love the outdoors just like me. One day I will have a farm for us and we will love it, life is so full of surprises and I like surprises. Oh there is this guy his name is Kelly, yup Kelly he really likes me but I don't think he is it, and I am not ready for a long term relationship, I want my life in order first I want to be moved out of my parents place and have a good education back-round, then I can meet the right man, I do want to date and have some fun dating, but I don't want to fall in love right now I am not ready. When I meet my soul mate I want to give him all of me, so when I am ready I can let him in. I believe that one day this will happen.

Dear Diary; June 13th, 93

Today I feel good about myself, and my self-esteem is getting boosted even more because that's the way I like to feel. In my life I have been to hell and back seen all kinds of people and the ones I find attractive are the ones who love Jesus and loves life, for what it holds for us. Life is a whole lot better when you love yourself, and it took me a long time to learn to love myself. Amen

---

Dear Diary; June 22nd, 93

Last night I had a really good time with mike I enjoyed his company and he is also very good looking, very intelligent for a 25 year old man, these kind of men are hard to find, we talked a lot and listened to each other and listened to music, I let him listen to what he wanted, then we told each other what we want and that we just want to be friends for now and that is it. I want to find out more about him before I get to involved, because I don't want to be hurt again and either does he. Today I had a very good day and I am spending more time with my wonderful girls. That's it, Amen

---

Dear Diary; June 24th, 93

I don't know if I mentioned that I was on a team before in my diary, but now I am and we are doing fine and have come a long way from there and we are having our graduation on Monday. We have finally made it through the God mother program we are the last ones to graduate in the family of woman, we went in April. And I know now that we can make it together, we can and I am not going to quit never, because I wont give up on myself and the kids. I cannot do that. I have made so many mistakes and I cant give up hope. So I wont do it again. I love them so much and I love myself now, and I cant give up on myself I am worth more then that. I love you Roxanne and Crystal, you 2 are the world to me, love mom. Amen

---

Dear Diary; June 26th, 93

Today I don't feel good inside physically or mentally, I know I am good and life is good. I think when you have friends and when you know what life is about, and that life isn't fare you can cope with what ever comes your way, also when you have something to live for and that I do, my two girls are the world to me and I only want the best for them, I want them to be happy and free and have a good life. I don't want them to go through the pain, and for them I know they will have their only struggles and go through some hard times in life. If life where easy we would move on and make life better for our selves. As long as I have God in my heart and the kids. Life will get better. Amen

---

Dear Diary; June 28th, 93

Today I had a pretty good day, it was a nice day, not to hot just nice, I feel bad though I was yelling at my kids and Roxanne got up and started crying and then I got mad at her and it only made matters worse I am sorry Roxanne for hurting you again, sometimes I just cant control myself. I love you Roxanne and Crystal sooooo much. And I am so sorry for hurting you two. Love mom Amen.

Dear Diary; July 18th, 93

Today I feel good and I have a lot of things on my mind. I am seeing this guy mike and I don't think he is the man for me, mainly because he is a non-believer, and he doesn't believe in Jesus and I want so much to have a man who believes in Jesus. I want my two girls to have two parents who believe not just one, I lived that way for many years. I want both my kids to live with 2 parents who are both Christians, not just one. Amen

---

Dear Diary; August 6th, 93

Today I was just reading some of the things I have written in this diary and I wonder about the things that I have said, pretty scary some of the things and some good to, I think I know who I want to spend the rest of my life with. I really like him and it has been 4 months now and I have done the woman's weekend and I feel great. Life is a whole lot better now and I can see clearly now. Oh and I won the lotto 649 $78,250.80 wonderful aye. I cant wait till Sunday the box lunch and also to see Bill again. He is so nice. I have decided to move into a 2 bedroom apartment and buy a new car and new furniture. I will save the rest of the money for my future. That's it for today. Amen

---

Dear Diary; September, 93

I haven't written in a long time and a lot has happen, I am completely moved into my new place and I have a brand new car and new furniture. I am very happy, a family has moved in up stairs. They seem very nice, they have 3 kids. My kids are in their new school and they like their teachers. I still don't have the man of my dreams but I am happy being single for now. It feels good to be out on my own again, and to have all new furniture and a new car, I can get places on my own now. Roxanne is maturing very much, almost to fast and I am not sure if I like it or not. I know we all grow up but its hard when your kids grow up so fast. Amen

---

Dear Diary; Dec, 5th, 93

Today its raining out and I feel good today, I have a new boyfriend, his name is Jeff although if he cant except my kids then this is not going to work out, I am not going to stay with him. I don't want to have a relationship with someone who doesn't want kids.

He probably doesn't even know if hes coming or going. Today is the day I am going to tell him this is not working and we will have to separate. I just want to be friends. I want to get things strait before we go away with them (Jeff and some friends). I know how I feel and I don't want to sleep with him or have any contact with him in that way. I have to tell him just so he knows how I feel and that I really don't want to have a relationship with him.

Paul is back in town, (A friend I have know for many years now) he is staying till Christmas is over with some friends, then hes going back to B.C. I will enjoy his company till he goes back to B.C. Amen

---

Dear Diary; Dec, 19th, 93

Today I quit the family of woman and for good reason I believe, the woman on the team don't think I should but I think who cares what they think any way. My life is fine, I have my own place and a car.

There is a mother who cares about me also knows.

I am going to try so hard to not yell at my kids, but sometimes they make me so angry.

I just feel like I quit on myself and the kids, I don't know what to do. Where do I go from here? Amen

P.S. I love you Roxanne and Crystal. xoxoxox
Love mommy.

Dear Diary; Jan 19th, 94

Today I feel great-full, my life has never been better, I have come a long way from last year and I do believe I have a lot of wisdom, I have learned form my mistakes, and don't regret any one of the decisions I have made. Because I have learned that we all make mistakes and I feel I have learned form mine, I am back with Jeff again I am happy, but I don't know if this is going to work, if he excepts my kids and we make it work then maybe it will work. My friend Grace is the one who introduced him to me, thank you Grace for thinking about me. Lets see how things go from here. I am happy with Jeff, I just don't want to be hurt again and I want whats best for my kids. About Jeff, he lives in Keswick Ont. He is a truck driver and makes good money, he own his own rig, he's is sensitive, kind, passionate and a real man. He has a very big heart.

He loves kids, dogs and cats and life. Thank you Jeff for excepting my kids, it means a lot to me.

Thank you God. Amen

Dear Diary; Thursday Feb, 24th, 94

It looks like a great future from here on in, the Lord has blessed me again with the man of my dreams and I am very happy with life right now. There is somethings I still have a hard time coping with, but I know in my heart that God is always with me. Jeff is a wonderful man and I am so glad he never gave up on me, I guess he new how much of a wonderful person I am and never gave up on me. So when you put to wonderful people together what do you get ? A great relationship. I guess that's it for now, (Note to self) remember Charlaine be the best you can be. God bless everyone. Amen

---

Dear Diary; Monday Mar, 14th, 94

I just woke up and I feel my relationship with Jeff is not going any where now, I was at his place from Tuesday night till Sunday, and on Saturday I was going to leave because he was going away on Sunday with Kim and Johnny again and he said, (I'II rephrase that question), he promised me he wouldn't be going away any more this year, that last weekend would be the last weekend he would be gone. Then he decided to go away on Sunday. I don't know any more, I really thought he wanted to settle down, I guess I was wrong.

I love Jeff a lot and I don't know what to do with out him, but what are the kids and me suppose to do just sit around all weekend without Jeff? Doesn't he realize how much this effects us, I think more me though, because I don't know what he's doing when he is gone away. We need to talk about things before they get worse then they already are. I just hope Jeff is willing to talk about it. I wish my mom was here for me to talk to, I need someone to talk to. Sometimes I wish I didn't fall in love because I hurt so much and I feel Jeff doesn't even care about me any more and that hurts, it really hurts, I wish I new who he was before I fell in love with him, I cant live this way I want to be together on the weekends as a family, the kids need a daddy not just a man in their life's and I need someone who's going to be there for me and understand me. I want to spend the rest of my life with Jeff but not like this where hes gone every weekend. I just want Jeff to understand how I feel, that's all. That's not asking to much is it? I love you Jeff and I need to be with you, why cant it be that he to would want to spend time with me too. That's it for now, I am crying so much I cannot read what I am saying. By for now.

Dear Diary; Thur, March 17th, 94

5:29 am

Today I am going to be a single mother, because that's what I am!! Until I get married and God only knows when that will happen. Also I realize that my life doesn't end here I still have a long way to go, so I should make the best of it while I am still alive. I will try to make each new day a good one and spend as much time with the kids as I can. They all grow up so fast and leave home, then it will be just me again. Also I want them to remember the good times we had, even though they don't have their daddy in their lives. I think they should still have a good loving relationship with me. After all they love me just the way I am. And I love them the way they are too. My beautiful little girls. Thank you Jesus for giving me two wonderful little girls. Amen

---

Dear Diary; Thur, Mar 17th, 94

I was just sitting here reading some notes I have written and I came across a pamphlet where Jeff, Grace, Dave, and oh of course Wesley to.(I went away without the kids). We went to Bell lake Lodge. That was the beginning of our relationship and I am so glad I made the decision to be with Jeff, I am very happy. The only thing is I am not with him as much as I wish I could be, but that's nothing really to worry about. He loves me just the way I am and I am a wonderful person, I love Jesus. And I wish the world would be a better place for us all.

"My thoughts today"

Wouldn't it be nice if Jeff and I went to Perry sound for our honeymoon? Yes, I know I would be very happy to do that even stay in the same lodge, well maybe not. I would want a honeymoon suite.

Also I was thinking (again) that even if we got married on the day we first met then go away snowmobiling for a week. ("To Bell Lake Lodge") That would be the happiest day in my life other then the day I got Baptized. I will talk to Jeff about it. By for now God bless and peace on earth.

P.S. Always remember Charlaine ("Be the best you can be")

Dear Diary; Sunday Mar, 20th, 94

Today I am very happy and glad to be with Jeff. Last night was the first time we went out together we went to the Keg and then a movie. Then we came home we made love and I was so happy. Then in the morning I made him breakfast in bed. He was really happy too. I know I made his day, I just hope I can keep him happy forever because I plan on spending the rest of my life with him. That's it for now. God bless and peace on earth.

I feel really good about how much I've grown with my children and with God, God has made such a difference in my life I didn't think I could have come this far if I didn't have God in my life, He is awesome. I love you Jesus and I plan to never leave Jesus again, I love you God and I hope Roxanne and Crystal always believe in Jesus and never leave the faith!! My hope is they follow you Jesus all of their days and forever Amen.

"FRIENDSHIP"

I said a prayer for you today and I know God must of heard, I felt the answer in my heart although He spoke not a word. (I knew you wouldn't mind)

I didn't ask for wealth or fame I asked for priceless treasures rare of a more lasting kind.

I prayed that He'd be near to you at the start of each new day, to grant you health and blessings fair and friends to share your way. I asked for happiness for you in all things great and all things small, but that you'd know His loving arms. I prayed the most of all. Amen

I guess I will start at where I am at now in my life and how far I have come, but first I want to say, that the real reason I am writing this book is because of (Barbara DeAngelis, MHD) (A book called Real Moments) this book gave me the inspiration to do what I always thought was not possible, I experienced many real moments in my life and one was to do with what I always thought not possible but now it is possible, and I am sure I will become afraid, and fear sometimes stops me in my tracks, but I am not going to let it stop me from writing this book if it takes me places I have never been before I think I will be glad after I finish it.

"I did it"

I finally made the choice to choose to do what i thought was always impossible (So to those things you always thought were impossible, do it don't wait, do it now) don't wait till the time is right or the place is right or anything else that stops you from doing what you "thought" you couldn't do.

Change it to (I CAN DO THIS.)

Dear Diary: 1:38 am April 6th, 94

I am not myself today, I have made Jeff mad at me and it was not my intention. I just wanted him to understand how I feel, its not that I don't trust him I do very much, Its just that I don't trust Sandy, I know how she is and I have only met her 2 times. She seems to me, to be a very sneaky person and I don't like people like that. If there where only more people like Jeff and I in this world, it would be a better place to live. I have to ask myself, is it worth it to talk to Jeff about this kinda stuff. When your in a relationship, you should talk about these kinda things. All I want is for Jeff to understand that's all, that's not asking to much is it? He probably thinks I don't trust him, I do. I don't trust her. I wonder if he is the one for me, sometimes I think he doesn't care for me as much as I do. I always want to be with him and I am not sure he feels the same way. I know we all need our space, I don't know any more I just hope when I talk to him he understands how I feel. I love him and I hope it all works out. Peace on earth...

As I write this book I wonder if it will sell, if I will be able to reach mothers out there who struggle with the same things as I do, its hard raising kids on your own, I have to be there for them and raise them and teach them wrong from right. I need to help them stay in school; and be responsible adults.

Life is a challenge and having 2 kids to raise makes it a little harder. I am happy I made the decision to leave there father and raise the kids myself, but I never new how hard it would be; I get so strung out and I feel like I lost myself in the mist of things. I often wonder how am I going to do this, I need help raising them, I wish I could find someone who is strong, forgiving, loving, understanding, caring and someone who understands what I am going through. As a Christian it can be very challenging to teach the kids about life and how it works, and help them through this life. Thank you God for giving me two wonderful girls, I am so grateful and blessed to have kids. Now to make the right choices for myself and them; Sometimes they are all I live for. Life has been really hard for me, I never had it easy, I came from a broken marriage and my father is an alcoholic and he abused my mother and put her in the hospital, on more then one occasion. I seen it first hand, and I was abused from babysitters to, Sometimes I wonder why God allows these things to happen to kids, like why let this happen, as he knows the out come and still lets it happen, I will never understand; I struggle with this on a daily basis. And I don't understand why?

Can I do this, can I raise healthy loving caring people who can trust and live a very productive lives, I hope I can. Lord help me to do this. Amen

---

Friday April 15th, 1994

The day before Crystals birthday, as I sit here wondering what tomorrow will bring, I hope happiness and joy but I feel sad inside and I don't know if Jeff really knows in his heart and soul if I am the one for him, I think I know he knows but something inside him wont tell me, I don't know maybe I am just thinking this and he really does want to be with me forever, I wish with my heart and soul he would talk about this with me. Jeff you mean a lot to me more then I have felt before, I don't think he really understands how much I love him, well its getting closer to Crystals birthday and I want to spend as much time with both girls because right now I am the only one that's really important person that's in their lives, they need me and I need them. I hope Jeff and the kids can be close, I know the kids want to get close to him, Roxanne said she loves him, she talks about him a lot, I don't want anyone to get hurt. Wow life is so hard...

February 1999

Day 1:Today I have decided that I am going to loose weight, Not to look good (although that will happen) but for my health, the doctor said my cholesterol levels are up a bit and my thyroid was a little UN-normal, so my health is at risk if I keep this up. So I am going to be dedicated to this with the strength from the Lord and for my children, after all they have lost their dad (Ron) they cant loose me too. Their Father was a dead-beat and never paid me any child support. And would disappear for months, one time I really did think he was dead, I never heard anything for like 6 to 9 months.

Starting today on February 8, 99

My prayer:

Dear Lord please give me strength when I really need it, In Jesus name I ask. Amen
Charlaine Simpson

Day: 2
Well I hope I can do good today, because I know last night I kinda slipped, I had one of those cakes that you buy from the store, and some pop too. I did good right up en till last night, anyway they say "we should look to the future" because the past is the past forever gone and the future holds a lot for me, I hope. I have to remember to, its only my second day I can't put myself down, and I just need to make the best of it.

My Thoughts:
I will talk about my hope, my hope is that I will do my best and be proud of what I have accomplished. And if I do really good I should do something nice for myself. Like buy a really nice outfit or a pair of shoes. Ya that's what i will do for myself. I feel good about my decision.

My prayer today:
I pray that Jesus would guide me and hold me when I cant see clear, and when things get real hard, this I pray in Jesus name Amen.

Day: 3
Today was OK I really did try not to eat to much, but I found that if I am not busy I get board and then I think of food, so I know I really need to keep busy and really try to do my best. I believe I

can do this with Gods help, I can. I hope each day gets better and when the nice weather comes I can do more things, like riding my bike and walking and swimming and playing with the girls.

My thoughts: I just hope I can stick with it and most of all keep the weight off. "Today I feel I can do it"

My prayers: Lord help me always remember I can do nothing with out you, also I pray that my health would be good and I will never have to weary about it again, also I pray for Roxanne and Crystal that they have a good healthy life style. In Jesus name I ask. Amen.

Psalm 92:14 September 5th, 96

Ugly Gremlins

"My dear heavenly Father, how can I ever express how great-full I am for your great care over me through the years, You have been so good, why then Lord do these ugly gremlins come into my thinking, I worry about someone or something hurting me or that they will hurt my children and this fear takes over my whole being, sometimes "only sometimes".

" Will I have to suffer with this for a long time before you take these feelings away? Oh God I pray you will take away my stinking feelings?

There now, I have expressed and verbalized them. Those ugly gremlins.

Lord, I now commit all these worries about these fears to you. I will claim the promise You have given me in Psalm 92.

That I shall still bring forth fruit in my own times of struggle, each time these fears come's up, I will go back and review this commitment until I have peace. I can trust you Lord with my worries and fears. I praise you my Lord. Thank you Lord.

Thank you Jesus.

"Help me Lord to keep my promise, To never give up hope to never give up on myself, and most importantly to never give up on my God.

I have a Promise to my God.
A promise to myself
A promise to my children.

Proverbs 18:22

He who finds a wife finds what is good.

And **Luke 14:28** " Suppose one of you wants to build a tower. Will he not first sit down and estimate the cost to see if he has enough money to complete it? For if he lays the foundation and is not able to finish it, everyone who see it will ridicule him.
Deuteronomy. 4:8 And what other nation is so great as to have such righteous decrees and laws as this body or laws I am setting before you today?

Malachi 3:8 Robbing God

"Will a man rob God? Yet you rob me. But you ask, how do we rob? In tithes and offerings".

Deuteronomy 8: 18

Do not forget the Lord, Remember the Lord your God, for it is he who gives you the ability to produce wealth, and so confirms his covenant, which he swore to your forefathers, as it is today.

"Money management"

Proverbs 17:13

If a man pays back evil for good, evil will never leave his house.

---

1 Corinthians 1-7

"Therefore you do not lack any spiritual gift as you eagerly wait for the Lord Jesus Christ to be revealed.

---

2 Corinthians 1-7

And our hope for you is firm, because we know that just as you share in our sufferings, so also you share in our comfort.
Amen

This is about Hamster's, Hamster are cute get a Hamster.

Marriage of the opposite sex! No
Don't marry someone who is of anger, or miens.
Have no sex at all before marriage.
Do not go into a business with an unbeliever.

Learn to walk away from buying!

I am a Sunday school teacher and I have a plan for the kids. The sun will rise, ask them (children) to go out in the morning sometime this week and watch the sun rise. Jesus is a Son and just as the sun rises in the morning every morning so shall He in your life, He is with you always. Amen

Next report back to me, on Sunday about what experience you had when you did this. OK

Give them a verse a month so they can memorize it by the end of the month.

They will receive something!

Tuesday Sept 2, 2008 6:57 am

I awoke with some anxiety about not having a job, about my life and all that is going on in my life.

Today I am making the choice to change my life for the better, I am not going to let circumstances get in my way of finding a good high paying job, and cleaning out my home of all the junk and giving stuff away that I don't need.

Today I am phoning the Landlord about my refrigerator to get a new one.

July 27th, 2008

Today I decided to not go to church and instead spend some quality time in Gods word.

I want so much to know my saver and learn more each day, to live for him and to do His will, Amen.

Lord Please help me, draw me closer and help me to help others. Lord please be with Roxanne, Crystal and all my family. Help us to help each other, for this is but for one purpose we sever here on earth. To love one another as our self's.

To honor God and keep the "Ten Commandments"

Thank you Jesus for always being there for me, and all those whom you care about.

Love mom, AKA Charlaine Amen

Monday July 28th, 2008

I awoke today at 2:30 am I am tired but cant sleep, so I got up and went for a short walk with Rob, we talked and it was nice.

Now I am relaxing down stairs in my basement Rec-room. I am going to read my bible and then nap for and hour or two, I will get up and shower and go out with Hilana we are going to a tour of an old train station it will be cool, cant wait.

Today I am going to clean my home and water my garden and walk the dog.

Friday August 1st, 2008

Today my grandson Noah comes over, I am always so happy to have him in my care even though it is only one day a week. I miss him and cant wait to see him. I am going to read my bible now and then lay down until Noah wakes me up. Today we are going out somewhere to enjoy the day together.

Aug, 11th, 2008 4:12 am

Today we are going out to look for caps for I-coke. Rob also wanted to show me around the university we where able to go inside and look around a bit, then we went to back outside and looked for bottle caps.

We are still struggling financially, I feel that its my fault, I need to pick up the slake and do more to get my income coming in. I am OK with this as I know God will help me. This is my hope. Thank you

---

Thursday Aug, 28th 2008 8:17 am

I am still looking for more work, I started looking more now and then when I first finished working as a daycare provider in my home. Since august 1st its been really hard, my first thought was maybe I should go on disability, cause I do find it very hard to find a job, yes even with all my skills. One that I will enjoy, 2 that I can work alone or with a team, 3 I don't like bosses hanging over my shoulder watching everything I do, to me that is so stressful and it makes me make more mistakes and it makes me nervous and I cant work good that way.

I am having a very hard time with this, Lord please help me find something that I can glorify your name and enjoy working there.

Sometimes I don't feel excepted, because of my disestablishes. I fear Lord please take my fears away. Amen

Sometimes I wonder about my life, what it could of been if I only Liston to My Lord, If only I hadn't been abused as a child and into my adult life, what would life be like, I think I am a pretty good person now, so if I wasn't abused I would be a much happier person; and I think I would of only gotten married once, cause I would of found the right guy with Gods help and direction, and I would have all my dreams, a home many kids, good health and a horse, I wish things could of turned out better. I know what they say that "life's what you make it"

But, what dose one do if they are put in a family that is abusive and babysitters abuse you. I still feel the pain till this day, and I often wonder WHY?

Another diary enter..

Dear Diary; Sunday May 1st, 9:45 am

I just got a call from Jeff and he said he doesn't want to be with me any more. I should of known it was coming we heaven-t been talking that much and Hes never here, I wanted it to work out. I haven't written about how I feel about Jeff and that it hasn't worked out for us. I wish it could of been a better relationship but I know now he isn't the one for me.

I've learned that men usually don't change, they only change if they choose not to, not cause we want them to. My kids need a daddy someone they can go to and feel loved by, I want someone to love me and the kids unconditional.

Gods peace...

Dec 5th, 17

Lets talk about the **"Holy Spirit"**

I have been reading the book of Romans and I am understanding more as I read and as the Spirit speaks to me through Gods word. I just need to learn to Liston better, make time to here Him and seek out the truth in my life. I know now that I am to try my best at doing good, and leaving the rest to God as He knows what I should do and will help me do it. In **Proverbs 20:27** talks about the Holy Spirit and that It was Gods desire to reunite the Holy Spirit with the human spirit so that they could again be one. Growing up I never really understood or even new that the Holy Spirit can speak to me or even help me, my mom never really taught me about such things, as she herself may not of know either. That is why so many go astray we don't know we are not taught, and if you are not taught then how are we to know. Like a flashlight you were designed to shine, but you can never shine with your own power. The Holy Spirit provides the power to produce the light, and once you shine as you were intended to shine, you will never be useless. amen

Also we read in Luke, John and Acts, that we are to continue in doing good works, in trying to help others find there way. It is through the Holy Spirit that we can find peace and harmony, it can be done and will; if you are willing. Amen

---

Dear Diary; May 25th, 94 5:50 am

I haven't written in a little while and there has been a lot of things that have happen to me, one I have let go of Jeff completely now, I know he wasn't the one for me, he probably would have never given to us what we needed anyway. I want a man that give us what we need, love and affection, a home and a save place to live. Someone who will be there for us, to understand us, Liston to us and love us unconditional, is there a man like that? I don't know. I hope when my kids get older they know how much and how hard I tried to find the right man to be there daddy. Their happiness is my number 1 priority and that I have tried my best. I hope I always have an open and honest relationship with them even through their teen years. My sister got married and I don't think its going to work out for them, considering the man he is. I guess its true what they say, you marry the man that resembles your father and our father was abusive. So we both married someone who abuses us. Sad but true. So I guess I am not the one to blame for the man I choose. But I am the one who chose him, so I guess I am the one who made the wrong chose. Another fact that is sad. I don't want my sister to go through the pain I have been going through, but I guess its not our plan.

My hope is they work through their problems and make it work for them. My hope is one day I can find a man that will love me unconditionally. Its getting closer to summer again and all the people showing more of their body parts, I need to get in shape again, its been to long and I have to stop putting it off. I only need to loose like 50 pounds. This time I am determined to keep it off. I want to live a long life and watch my kids grow up and see my grand kids and great grand kids.

That's it for today.

Some times I hate life, I hate the evil in this world we live in. Why do we have to have all this pain and anger and mails, people fighting and hating. I am so tired just so tired of trying to help my children, Lord I am tired of living. How long oh Lord, how long do I have to suffer, how long. I am tired and worn out, can life ever be good for me? Will I ever be happy? Will I ever be debt free? Will I always be pour? Dose life ever get better?

These are hard questions to express. To answer even.

I do believe God can answer these and help me understand. If I can help just one person and help them to come to know Jesus, then I have done a good job. Amen

Dear Diary; Thursday June 23rd, 94

Today I am pissed off, yesterday Missy and I went to Sutton to see her mother and on the way Missy said lets go see Jeff, I said OK, So after we go to her mothers we went to see Jeff, we got there and know Jeff but his friend Mike was there so we stayed for a beer just as we where leaving Jeff calls, so mike is talking to him, and just as we are leaving Mike says Jeff want to talk to me, So I say OK let me talk him, the minute I get on the phone his ex is yelling in the back round at me saying rude names to me and I have never even met her and that makes me mad, and how does she know about me when we have never met officially, Jeff has told her about me, he must of said some bad things cause why would she be yelling at me. I don't even know her. I am not happy with Jeff why would he do that? He also told me he would never move to Scarborough when we where together, and now hes moving in with her and its in Scarborough, go figure aye, it doesn't make sense to me. I think he just never got over her, and now he gets the chance to move in with her, I guess he thinks its a second chance with her. I will never go back to him and I cant believe he wanted to talk to me with her there, men... I wont take this any more. Wait till he phones me I will give him a mouth full. Like doesn't he think, shes right there with him and he wants to talk to me, DA. Peace out.

So another day, another dollar, I am sitting here at my desk and wondering why the heck cant I get this book done, why do I have such trouble keeping my faith and keeping promises to myself. I am only doing this book to help people mainly young woman who are just starting out in this life and need direction, I often wonder why things work out the way they do, don't you? I think about this great big world we live in, and I cant believe I am so small to it, so delicate and I do make a difference even if people don't understand all of me, they can maybe appreciate what I have to offer them, my experience in this life has been hard but I do have so many days that are filled with joy. I have to keep looking for the future cause nothings going to stop me now, I am going to make my dreams come true and (with Gods Help) I can. You know sometimes I think to much and wish I could just shut my brain off it would be great, I should invent something like that, NOT... I will be the best I can be and I will be happy with it. I will continue to strife for my dreams and ant nothing going to hold me down, I have a great and mighty savour who understands me more then I understand my self. I am going through this journey and I cant wait till I see whats around the corner. I want to go places see places and do things most people might not do, I am an adventurous person, I am not afraid of going out there and doing it myself, I am a strong and good person, I can make a difference and I will. You know how the saying goes, "feel the fear and do it any ways". I am doing that, through my book, I am going to help as many people to the Lord as I can and if it means exposing myself to the world so be it, I will keep going. I will not let fear take over me, Lord help me to be strong and carry on.

Thursday Aug, 14th, 2008 7:20 am

Today I awoke thinking about camping, I love to camp and be out doors and among the nature.

Today I have to clean the van and pack it for camping, we will camp this year for one night at Pioneer Park. This place is great for swimming, canoeing and nature walks. Three of the things I love to do. I am so looking forward to camping I am glad I am with someone who loves to camp to.

Lord thank you for the nature and all it has to offer us, may we continue to take care of our lands, Thank you lord for my husband and the kids and my grandchild Noah. Amen

Going back to all the stuff in my past is painful for me and it will be painful for you to, just don't let that stop you, I mean how can people stop me from having my dreams, I guess in life people are so, I don't know so proud maybe, I just knew I could do this if I just Liston to God and not what other people want for me, or want me to do. I mean even from the get go when your a child people are telling you what to do with your life right, and mom and dad are trying to help us but they really don't know our journey only we know what we really want, All I ever wanted was to be loved, to be held to feel like I am somebody, not just anybody but some buddy.. I am going through some changes again and If I don't express how I feel then I get stressed out, and I feel like a caged lion, that needs to freed. It maybe that I just have always been a wild child and that is OK with me, I have learned to deal with my own demons and keep going, never give up. I say this to myself never give up hope. I will be open and honest with myself first then I will be open and honest with everyone else. My dreams seem so far away but I can be all that I want to be. I am going to enjoy this long weekend as it has so much. BBQ and family are what makes me happy, the simple things in life make me happy, but the huge things in my life make me excited.

Its 2:31 am and I am still up, sipping my water and thinking about everything. I have a cold today and have been sick with the stomach for some time now, its been so long I wonder if its something really bad going on, having diabetes isn't fun, and taking all these pills makes me feel sick. I hate the pills. I will go for now. Till we meet again. I hope this book makes you feel special and loved.

I woke today around 3am. Sometimes I wonder how I do it, how can one person go on so little sleep, but I have done this most of my life, I love to sleep don't get me wrong, but When you suffer with this sleep problem you learn to cope, and deal with it. one one day at a time, I think WHY, why do things happen, why do we feel like were running a race. Because we are, I will run this race and I will win, I will continue this race until the end, and if it takes me my whole life to get this book written then so be it, but I am never giving up, I have a hope and a dream. Well I have many dreams and I sometimes wonder if they will come true, You see I have had so many road blocks its not funny, and my life is no bowl of cherries. I get stuck in situations and I feel that I sometimes cant get out of, like in a bad relationship. Lets go there lets see where I can see where I went wrong.

Sept,17th 1994

How I feel today with myself and my children, today I feel good about how much I have grown, with my children and myself. God has made such a difference in my life. I plan to follow Jesus all my life. To Roxanne and Crystal, always believe, never give up hope, and keep your chin up.

I said a prayer for you this morning, I know God must of heard: I felt the answer in my heart although He spoke not a word. I didn't ask for wealth or fame (I knew you wouldn't mind) I asked for priceless treasures of a more lasting kind.

I prayed that he would be near to you at the start of each new day, to grant you health and blessings fair, and friends to share your way. I asked for happiness in all things great and small but that you'd know his loving care. I prayed the most of all. Author I don't know.

September 5th, 1996

This poem is from me, I came up with it.

"My dear heavenly father how can I ever express how grateful I am for your great care over me through the years, You have been so good to me, why then Lord do these ugly gremlins come into my thinking? I worry about something or someone hurting me, or my children and this fear takes over my whole being. Will I have to suffer with this for a long time before you take these feelings away? There now I have verbalizes them, those ugly gremlins"

Lord I now commit all these worries about these fears to you. I will claim the promise you have given me in Psalm 92.

That I shall still bring forth fruit in my own time of struggle. Each time these fears come up for me, I will go back and review this commitment until I have peace, I can trust you Lord with all my worries and fears, I praise you Lord. Thank you Jesus, Amen.

Following God:

First: Always fight your battles on your knees.
When you do you will always win.

Second: Decide before hand that your going to obey God, regardless what happens.

Third: find your strength in God.

Forth: Refuse to run away, know matter how bad things get.

Fifth: Guard your lips, we can do damage with them.

Sixth: Be alert to growing weary, when the battles grow long.

Seventh: Stay on the path to victory, you must see that everything that happens comes from God himself.

For God know what we can endure:

Sunday February 21st, 1993

Lets talk about how we feel and what we want in life, when I was at church today I talk to Pastor Roy, he asked me a few questions. Some where surprising and some I new where coming my way.

Life changes a lot, some things we go through are very difficult. As a child we learn to except who we are and what is around us, as we get bigger (around 5 years old) we learn to like our self's and ask questions and try to find direction. As we get even older (10 years old) we begin to be our own self's and have control of whats going on around us, so you see we learn from a very young age how to control people, places and things, we all learn this! We never stop learning till we die, we all have a fear of someone or something, Right. You once asked me to tell you how I feel on paper now is the time, I don't know if you will understand what I have said but I hope you have some idea of how I feel, see, think, and understand, for Jesus is the only way to live and the only one who loves me and cares about me, even though I have so many bad habits and many other things wrong with me. I have done some pretty bad things in my life. God wants us to Liston to his word so we can learn the better way of doing things, because we tried our way and that didn't work, we tried our parents way and that didn't work either. My life has been a battle up to this point. Please keep a open mind. I will start from the beginning, I lived in metro housing and grew up there until I was 5 years old. I don't quit remember much at that age, then we moved to another area of housing I grew up there for a few years, I have very few memories, I only seem to remember the good ones and some of the bad ones, like when I was riding my bike and I fell down and scrapped my knee. I was then brought to this place we now live (173 Horsely hill Dr). I remember a lot of good times here, but they where not always good, I had to learn at a very young age to be responsible, and that to me was good. We are all Gods children. I was about the age of 13 when I started using drugs, for me it was a way out of all the issues that I was dealing with, little did I know it would lead to more problems.. I started not listening to my parents, not coming home when I was suppose to, lying to them, stealing from them coming home drunk and not knowing where I was who I was with or how I would get home. My mom was my best friend just before I started doing drugs and I lost that and everything else that went with it. We use to go shopping together and that stopped, My life went down hill even though I never seen it coming, I thought life was great, drugs do that to you. You think your doing great and nothing can stop you. But inside your eating away at yourself, bad thoughts return and the more I smoked weed the more I felt better, it took away all the bad feelings.

I was brought up in a half Christian home, (I say half because my dad is a non believer) and I became a Christian at the age of 12, I prayed to God to help me and come into my heart and renew it, bless me father. I may of been mentally aware but not physically. I was afraid (we all do the things we do, because we are afraid), we feel rejected, neglected, we want people to love us so we try harder to make these people love us, not thinking about them. I moved out at the age of 14 years old.

This was a big step, I learned at a very young age to live on my own and how to grown up, to cope with life., I was drinking beer and smoking pot, I learned a lot out there, I know now how bad it is, I learned how to pay bills, pay rent and pay for the things I needed and wanted. I also learned how to love, I learned how to have kids. In life there are a lot of changes and I learn how to cope, I had to. For me my life was changing all the time, when you find out who you are, where you want to go and how to get there,. You just have to act on it and don't stop. I am still young and have a lot to learn and growing up to do,. God has always been there for me and has never let me down He just keeps trying to help me. Pastor Roy has been a blessing to me and my girls, and I will always remember him and his family. I did a lot of soul searching for someone like Roy and now that I found him and his church, I will never leave. His wife Belinda is a saint, He couldn't of married anyone better. In Gods eyes we are all His children. I will never leave such a caring Church like this one, May God be with us all. May we look back on our lives but don't live there, May life bring us where we want to go.

When I first started to write this letter I had know idea how it would come out like the way it did, but I am glad because I have said what I wanted to say and I feel a whole lot better. Here I go with another change. I have had a lot going on in my life. Some that I could cope with and some not. Every time I went through a bad time in my life I came out with something good and noble and have more knowledge. For me that is the only way to learn, to experience it. To grow through it. We sometimes need to go though rough times to come out of it with something good that we can bring with us through out out lives. Thank you for taking the time out and really listening to me and trying to understand me better. I hope this helps each and everyone who reads this letter.

P.S. To Roxanne and Crystal for teaching me about life and how to be a good mother and for being my friend. Love always Charlaine (mom)

April 23 2002

Respect:

Lets talk about it, do you know what the word means? Lets look it up. An attitude of deference, admiration or esteem, regard, the state of being. To have an attitude towards, show or have respect for elders, to pay proper attention to.

Do I want to be respected {Yes} and how do I get respect, by first respecting the other person.

So I am going to respect all my family, friends, and coworkers. And the one person I love the most, my husband Rob. I am going to start today yes today not tomorrow. I am glad I talked about that one little word, called respect. It maybe hard for you and may require a great deal of letting go, letting go of your ego, your pride and the things that hold you back, and hold you down. What ever the case may be. You deserve to be respected, loved and cared for, and so do they. Thanks for taking the time to read my book and not giving up on yourself and your loved ones. You have come one more step to becoming the person you want to be, the person God wants you to be.

Sensitivity: A noun

A strong word, one who deeply loves, one who cares. The quality or condition of being sensitive.

Can be easily offended. When we think about other peoples feelings we put them first, we care for even those that do us wrong, but we can become UN-sensitive to those who hurt us, because we hurt deeply and we don't want to be hurt, like it says in the bible. Do onto others as you would want done to you. Most of us want peace and harmony.

December 19th, 1993

Dear God;

This is Charlaine Simpson you know who I am and what my name is going to be Pridham now.

One thing I don't understand is why do we have to go through so much pain and suffering, and how much of it can we handle, I don't think I can handle any more. How much of it can you handle?

I have been through so much already and I am only 25 years old. Cant we learn in life what we need to learn without the pain and suffering, are we just to stupid to learn, maybe that's whats the matter is, we are to stupid to know how to do it right the first time.

Dear Diary: Thursday April 28th, 94

As I sit here thinking about my life, I often wonder what will be around the corner waiting for me I know in my heart it will be someone better, "I believe that" but for now I am having a hard time leaving the past behind me, because Jeff is the best I have ever had, he never hit me or abused me in any way, he just hurt my heart by leaving, I want a man to spend time with me and my kids, that's what is so important to me. I might add that building a relationship and spending time with the kids, He never had any kind of relationship with my kids, he doesn't want kids I guess, So I realize I need someone who loves me and my kids, we are a package and If you don't love my kids and want to be with them then its not worth it. The kids are all I have and they keep me going, if it weren't for them I don't know where id be now, they are my life. I have to tell him the truth about how I feel and tell him I am not playing games any more, I cant go on like this I have to tell him it is not working and that we cannot get back together (its been an on and off relationship) I know its going to be hard but I have to be strong for them and me, I know this will hurt us but I have to leave him behind and find my one true love.

You know sometimes life hurts, the things that have happen to me in this crazy life of mine, I think about things and I want to write it out, but usually I get those thoughts when I am in bed and cant sleep, so I lay there and think about what I want to say or how I feel, but if I keep on trying to sleep I find myself thinking I need sleep I haven't had much sleep in a while, so I just keep thinking about this book and how much I just want it to be done, its been so long and hard to keep going with my book, will people even like my book, will it sell, am I wasting my time, No. I know I need to keep going with this book of mine, I think I can and I want to help many people. Although my target is young moms, single moms, and anyone in between. I will get my book published and I hope I can make a real difference in your life's, I hope I haven't bored you yet and my hope is when you have read my book, that you would pass it on to someone you might know who could benefit from it. Then my job is done, that's the whole reason for writing this book I just want to help as many people as I can, to give you hope, to help you along your life's Journey, This is my Journey one that I hope helps me, (I wanted to give hope and joy back into your life and If

I have done that then I have done my job) I have run the race and fought the good fight, Now I just have to keep going and not loose hope, to keep pushing forward, and not giving up on myself, You can do this for yourself. Right...
Another diary

Dear Diary: Nov 12th, 1995

Its been a good but tough year, we all have come a long way, and I believe the lord has changed us. I guess there will always be change in ours lives and I believe that it has made me a better person. I am tried going to bed. Good night

Dear Lord; I do hope I find the right man who can take care of me and my kids and I hope I find him soon, because the kids are getting older and they need a daddy. I want to choose the right one and I have had a hard time finding Mr. Right. I don't want them to feel lonely and with out a daddy.

Lord God I love you and respect you with all my heart, and I am asking for forgiveness for my sins please forgive me Jesus for I am a sinner and I just want to be excepted and loved by my family, I know you love me and my parents love me, I made so many bad choices I think they cannot forgive me.. Lord God you will always be in my heart and my children will always mean the world to me.

Thank you God for giving me such beautiful children. Thank you Amen.

Dear Diary: Monday May 29th, 1995

Its been awhile since I have written, I have been to busy to write in my diary, still living in this 2 bedroom basement apartment.

Its OK for now but the girls are growing up so fast, and they will need their own bedroom. I am finished school now (went back for my grade 12) and I am going to start looking for a job by August because the kids will be going back to school, man this single living thing is hard, all I want for my girls is happiness.

I will have to look for someone to take care of them on P.D days and holidays. I realize I cant live with out Jesus, to keep me on track, Know one knows me like you Jesus.

Dear Roxanne and Crystal, my hope is you succeed in life. You are smart and intelligent, (I guess you get that from me) One thing I hope you will never give up on, is your kids, never. I hope you girls meet a nice man and a respected man, one who will take care of you. I pray for you both all the time and I know the Lord heard me, he always answers prayers, Maybe Yes, maybe no, and maybe wait.

Love mom.

How to pick a partner. Spiritual Compatibility.

Proverbs 21: 19, 2 Corinthians 6: 14-15.

Deuteronomy 6:1, 2

Building a Case:

2 people come together and have the same blueprint, A mutual blueprint. When 2 people come together and have an understanding of each other.

Always remember that Jesus comes first, and that he can except that.

Let the Holy Spirit come into my life and do its work, God wants us both to be in the house of Jesus, He wants us both to love and honor each other. Teach your children about God.

A mutual parenting passion **Deuteronomy 6-9**

Every night talk to your kids about spiritual things and tell them about what to do, and pray for them.

Always remember it doesn't matter what happens to them so long as they believe in the Lord, treat them how you would want to be treated. When things go wrong and they do, that's when Jesus will be there more then ever. Serve the way you want to be served Teach me Lord how to teach my kids. Amen

---

February 5th, 17 8:05 am

So today I got a message on my wall on Facebook and I realize that I am not alone in this fight to survive on this earth, sometimes I feel alone but deep down I know I am not alone, God sees everything and knows everything, we just have to trust in Him with our lives, sometimes I get so sad and all I think about is that life is not worth living, but I know that is not from me or from God; the devil wants us to do crazy stupid things and if we just trust Jesus with our lives He will make it right again for you, he will and does understand everything we are going through, If God allows it then He knows we can handle it, I never really understood what that meant until I gave my life to Him, Jesus made us, and only wants the best for us.

I often wonder if I didn't have God what would I do, how would I cope, and then I think about all those people out in the world struggling just to get by, and they have know one they can trust, and life seems hopeless, well I am here to tell you there is more, much more to you and God wants you to know that. He wants you to be free, to feel again and be somebody, we are all here on this earth to make a difference, and if we trust our hearts enough to let Jesus in then our lives will never be the same, we will be a changed person. I trust you Jesus and I want you to be the centre of my life, please help me and guide me on this journey and please give me peace, amen

---

The Ten Commandments
Deuteronomy 5: 6

1. You shall have no other Gods before me
2. You shall not make yourself an idol.
3. You shall not misuse the name of the Lord
4. Observe the Sabbath day by keeping it Holy
5. Honor your father and mother
6. You shall not murder
7. You shall not commit adultery
8. You shall not steal
9. You shall not give false testimony against your neighbor.
10. You shall not covet your neighbor's wife.

These are the Ten Commandments the Lord proclaimed in a loud voice to your whole assembly.

If you keep these commandments it will go well with you.

If you break one you broke all, But there is hope God can forgive you and then you must tern and walk away from those sins, do know more. Ask God to help you and he will if you ask with a sincere heart, He will do it.

Be careful, do what the Lord God tells you to do, read His word meditate on His word, spend time in His word; the Bible will help you grow as a Christian and help you to live a life God intended you to live. Go in peace...

But because of his great love for us, God, who is rich in mercy, made us alive with Christ even when we were dead in transgressions — it is by grace you have been saved. Amen

---

Ephesians 2:4-5

Another diary entire...

Dear diary: Tuesday, Aug 2, 94

Today I had a good day in Hastings, where my grandmother lives for the summer, but shes not there this summer. My mom and dad are staying there for 2 weeks. anyway I came home today and the kids said they had a good weekend, I had a good weekend with them to; now I am sitting here thinking about how much I trust in the Lord Jesus and I know in my heart there is a man out there for me and I know that's not all he has in store for me and my two kids, but my heart aches for Jeff hes the one I think about a lot and is the one who help me realize a lot of things about myself, I am a good person and I can love someone very much and let go of the past, I can let go and still love him, one day I will write a book about my life, and maybe that's what I will call it (My life.)

Thank you Lord Jesus and mom and dad.

God bless and peace on earth. Amen

As I sit here and think about things, I wonder if I am making the right decisions and doing the right things, I think with my depression I sometimes get caught up in my own world I forget there are people out there who are struggling and as I struggle to make sense in all that I am and all that I do, I just think; sometimes I have so many issues that I am dealing with, will I always struggle?

I will never give up on my dreams, I cant. And I wont. I just have to keep my faith, go to church and pray always.

Life can knock you down, but we have to just get back up, and keep going I cant give up, I am a strong person and I can do this, I can finish this book and my hope is that one day when this gets published I will know that I am done, and that I finally finished what I started. And if I can help one person my job is done. Writing this book has taken me a very long time to do, I always thought know one will want to read what I have to say, so I give up on my self, not any more I will run the race and I will be victorious because I have a great God who helps me and gives me hope.

I sometimes think what will the world will think of me, there are so many personal things in my book that I always said will stay within me, I will never share my story, but I realize that I am not the only one who struggles to make it through this life. I am not alone in my pain and that I am not alone in trying to make ends meet, I will keep going.

I am so upset right now I am trying to keep going and I am trying to make the best of what I have and it is so hard, I am upset because I miss my dad, I am on a journey to find him but I have little resources and I am so afraid he might be dead or worse, I miss him Terribly. I have been searching my whole life for him, he abandoned me at age 5, I just want him to know that I still love him and miss him, I want my questions answered and maybe I will feel better maybe I wont have this feeling that someone will abandon me again, So I tend to run from conflict and I have never really know how much I am really loved, I mean my whole life all I ever wanted was to feel excepted loved and cared for, I am struggling daily with my demons and I know deep down God will always be there, He will always understand me fully, he will never abandon me, he will never hurt me like all the men in my life, Lord please help me get this right and to make this out come be good, I just need you lord right now please help me in this search, help me find the answers to all my questions, I afraid he might be dead and I didn't get to him in time. Time is running out and I have know more resources, I have tried so many thinks, I have put it on Facebook and talked to so many people and I have been praying and hoping that some day I will find you dad, until then I will always and forever be thankful for all the experiences in this life.

Another diary entire...

Dear Diary: Nov, 12th, 1995

Well its been a good but tough year for me we all have come a long way and I believe the lord has changed us once again, I guess there will always be change, and I know He is making and moulding me to make me a better person.

My daughter Roxanne has her big sister right now and she is so very happy with the match, her name is Ann and she seems to me to be a good person, although she doesn't go to church I think she believes in God. I do hope that Roxanne would bring her to (maybe one day) church. Maybe Roxanne will ask her to go with us, there is always hope. I believe that with Roxanne having a big sister now she will get better and her self-esteem and self-motivation will keep building and that Roxanne will feel better about herself. I don't know what Roxanne wants to do for work in this life , but I have hope that it will come to her and she will work her hardest at achieving it. Also I am involved in a group and I am hoping they can help me with my issues, I believe they are helping me to stay in my heart and to accomplish all that I can in this crazy life here on earth. Thank you Lord for helping me and my two beautiful girls. Crystal is getting better to she is really trying to stop sucking her thumb, but it will take time. She is so prouses to me, Crystal is an angle from Heaven, and I believe all the children are sent to us are from heaven. I think Crystal is going to be good at what ever she desires to do. Crystal is the other half of my brain, she always reminds me of things I forget.

Amen Thank you Jesus. God bless and peace on earth!!

P.S Roxanne and Crystal You are my angles sent to me from heaven, I love you more then you will ever know.

Another dairy entree...

Dear Diary: April 6th, 1996

Today I awoke at 5am and I am thinking again and reflecting on my life, how far I have come, the long road I have travelled and I don't think I would have made it with out my lord. He is my rock my light onto my path. When nights get so cold and I am lonely I need Him more, Lord you are so wonderful to me. About a week ago I have come to realize how much I do love Jesus, He talks to me and He walks with me until I am his own, and He talks to me through music, I know because I have asked him to speak to me through song and in a way that I will know (without a doubt) that it is Him. I have never felt better in my whole life, I just want to keep that feeling forever and I never want to get so angry again in my life. I find when I get angry and mad my heart grows hard, and when your in love with Jesus your heart feels so worm and light. I sing out a love song, just to let Him know how much I love Him. I have to say I cant live without my group, I believe they have helped me get back on my feet and see where my higher calling is, and that community means so much to me, just to help out, like volunteering. When I volunteer I feel the love and that's what matters to me, making a difference in my life. I am still in this basement apartment and i cant wait to move, the girls need their own rooms. I have to remember that my kids are a gift from God and I have to except and love them just the way they are.

I have many dreams and I do hope they come true, One of them has come true and that is I wanted to compassionately love the Lord with all my heart. I got that dream last night. I feel like I have accomplished so much in my life, its time I grew up. I had to grow up on my own, I moved out so young, and became a mommy at such a young age 17. I had to grow up and be a woman, and I think that is part of growing up in it self. My hope is my children don't grow up to fast, my hope is that they both meet a good Christian man to live with them and they live a happy life. I don't want them to go through any kind of hurtful and painful separation.

Today is going to be fun we have lots of things planned today, and tomorrow is the dedication for the girls, I am so proud of them and of myself, I want so much for my church to see that there is hope for single mothers and that we can make it though tough times. And I have the Lord within my heart forever. I know He has always been there I just didn't realize it until last night, He really does love me. Thank you Jesus thank you. God bless and peace on earth.

With Love in your heart anything is possible.

Amen

Another diary entry:

Dear God,

Hi you know who this is Charlaine Simpson, soon to be Pridham. One thing I don't understand is all the suffering we have to go through and why all the pain, and how much of it can one endure, I don't know if I can handle any more suffering, I have been through so much already and I am only 25 years old with two girls of my own. Cant we learn in this life what we need to learn without going through the pain or are we just to stupid to know it. Maybe that's whats the matter, we dont get it and have a hard time understanding, Lord God I hope I can find the right man for me and my kids, soon I hope they are getting older and they might not except a man. They might get use to not having a dad and that is sad, I want them to feel the love of a daddy. God I love you and respect you with all my heart and I ask for forgiveness of all my sins, please forgive me Jesus for I am a sinner and I just want to be loved by you and my family, I know they love me and you do to, but I guess because I did so many bad things, I think they cannot forgive me. I know you God will forgive me and I know you will always be in my heart and the children will always mean the world to me, Thank you God for giving me two beautiful girls. God help me raise them to be strong independent Christian adults. Amen

Love mom

Filter #1

Is this prompting truly from God.

Simply ask God the father: Is this message truly from you?

Ask myself is this true what has been said, take your time and resort to the bible and in prayer to discern right from wrong, ask is it consistent with your character. Keep praying till the answer comes. This may take a few times so we need to be open to here the Holy spirit speak. Prayer is best done alone in your private space so that you can here His small voice. God is calling you...

Filter #2

Next run the prompting through the scripture filter.

Ask my self if I could imagine Jesus taking whatever action I am considering taking, If I cant envision Jesus following suit I fear my wires somehow must have gotten crossed. Read **Galatians 5: 16 and 26**

A message that contradicts scripture are not from God.

Filter #3 Is it wise?

To be wise in all our ways. To be wise in all our dealings.

Filter #4

Is it in tune with your own character?

Filter #5

What do the people you most trust think about it.

Read **Proverbs 11:4**

When ever I sense that God is speaking to me, find two or thee veterans (Christ followers) preferably people who know you well and who are further down the spiritual path that you are. Take time to describe the situation to them in detail, humbly ask them. “Do you think God really spoke to me? is this the voice of God I am hearing or in your estimation did I get my wires crossed?

A book by Mother Teresa. “Come be my light”
Check it out.

The truth about salvation **Titus 3:5**
Salvation is a gift from God by Gods grace alone.

Romans 10:13

Everyone who calls on the Lord will be saved.

John 1:12

Yet to all who did receive Him to those that believed in His name, He gave the right to become children of God. Amen

Read **1 John 5:12**

When life seems to be pulling you down or things in your life are causing you pain, reach out to God. Ask and it will be given onto you, Seek and you will find, knock and the door will be open. Jesus will calm the storm in your life, if you just let him in, He will move that mountain that is in your way, even if you only have faith as small as a mustard seed, even if where you are right now seems scary or dark, God wants to bring you into the light and give you hope, don't give up God has a better plan in mind. All you have to do is just ask and He will fill your heart with Joy, an unspeakably Joy, You can do this, don't give up. Jesus will calm the storm in your life, just take that chance; what do you have to loose, and He will help you up out of that slimy pit. " He will catch you" Just fall into His loving arms and He will be there, He loves you, He wants to give you peace.

Sometimes when you feel like you lost all hope and you don't know why, you want to just give up, Just give your life over to Him who knows every hair on your head. Every tear that runs down your cheek.

O Lord how majestic is your name in all the earth.

O Lord how Majestic is your name, O Lord, we praise your name.

Prince of peace, mighty God, O Lord God Almighty... Amen

Another diary entree...

Dear Diary: Wednesday, June 21st, 1995

Sometimes I think I write just because I need to express how I feel or whats going on in my life, right now I feel very lonely and upset, the kids just don't Liston sometimes and doing this is very hard I have been doing it for so long 7 years by myself and I don't even have my mother, she seems to never really be there for me, I just wish I had someone who cares about me and someone who understands about my feelings, I need someone who I can love and will love me unconditionally someone I can talk to someone I can just be myself with. I feel better now that I wrote this down, although sometimes I think I am going to loose it and end up in the hospital. I am leaving to BC and I do hope I have a good time, because If I dont I probably wont go back. I plan on moving in the summer so the kids can have their own rooms and so I can live a better life other then living in a basement apartment. Well that's it God bless and peace on earth. Love mommy.

Another diary entree...

Dear Diary: Nov, 12th, 1995

Well its been a good but tough year for me, I have come a long way and I believe the Lord has changed me, I guess there will always be change in our home. I believe that, I know change is good but tough at the same time.

Roxanne has her big sister now she is so happy to have her. I am so happy she has someone else to talk to and have a good friendship with. Her name is Ann and she seems to be a good fit, I don't think she goes to church But I do believe she believes in God. My hope is that Roxanne will invite her to church one day. Maybe Roxanne will ask her to come to our church. I know with Roxanne having a big sister now, she will get better she will get better at her self-esteem and self motivation. I don't know what Roxanne wants to do for work in her life, but I do hope that it will come to her what she'd like to do for work. And I hope she will work her hardest at achieving it. Also i am involved with a group called "The family of woman" and I believe that they are helping me to stay with my heart and to accomplish all that I can in this life here on earth. Thank you lord for helping me and my two girls.

Crystal is getting better, she really is trying to stop sucking her thumb, but I know it will take time she is my angel sent from heaven. And I believe that all children are sent form above and given to us to take care of. I think Crystal is the other half of my brain, she always reminds me of things I forget.

Nov, 24th 17

Reading Acts, if you want to get your bible so you can refer to what i am saying and then understand.

So it was with the Holy Spirit that we understand, **Acts 15:6-11** God who knows the heart, showed that he excepted them by giving them the Holy Spirit, just as he had done for us, He made know distinction between us and them, for He purified their hearts by Faith. We believe it is through the grace of our Lord Jesus that we are saved, just as we are. So what I got from reading **Acts 15:6** is that they now longer needed to be circumcised, we are excepted by faith in God.

I pray that you and I will continue to believe and help those that are lost, find hope and peace with our Lord God. My hope is you will understand what God wants you to do in your life, from here and now I want only good for you and your family.

Thank you Jesus for excepting me just the way I am and for helping me understand your word, Lord help these people who are reading my book to understand your great love for them. Lord they picked up this book and thought it would be a good read, and I hope it will give them some hope to never give up on there dreams, Lord God you know them and understand their circumstances and you alone will give them a peace and Joy. Amen

Every day is a journey and my hope is that your journey will be good, and that you will be faithful in what your calling is. Even in the hurt we can come and God will give us rest.

Thank you Jesus, God bless Peace out.

Love mommy

Saturday December 2, 17

We read, **Romans 10: 9-10**

That if you confess with your mouth,

"Jesus is Lord" and believe in our heart that God raised Him from the dead you will be saved. For it is with your heart that you believe and are justified, and it is with your mouth that you confess and are saved. Amen

Faith comes from hearing the message and the message is heard through the words of Christ.

Amen

Let us continue to do the right things and follow our Lord God, all the days of our life's, we must confess every day because we struggle with the sinful nature on a daily basis, so we must continue to do right. Ask, Seek and knock. For there is hope there is always hope.

I love you Lord God and I want to live for you alone, and all things will come to me because I trust you with all my heart, I am set free... Amen

How to pick a partner: Read

Proverbs 21:19 2 Corinthians 6:14-15 Deuteronomy 6:1-2

I am reading one of Charles Stanley's books and I am understand him more and I feel closer (even though I have never met him) Closer to knowing him, he is a strong Christian. I hope I can be a strong Christian woman in my life. Amen

Go in peace and spread the word, talk, Liston and be still before the Lord God almighty. Amen

---

Friday Oct 13th, 2017

I am thinking that I should end this chapter of my life and start a new one, until then or until me meet again or shall I say, when you want to or need someone you can trust, someone who you can confined in (Ask Him who knows all), every hair on our heads, every scar on our body's, everything, He who seeks finds and he or she who ask will be given on to you, The Lord is a great start,.

Let us pray together...

I have run the race I have tried and failed and I am giving my life to you Lord Jesus, I want and need you right now, please come into my heart and help me with what ever it maybe, I give my life to you. Amen

---

Dear God, Friday Jan 19th,18

I am struggling with the loss of my brother Scott He was a good man, but he did have a drinking problem (I think he never realize) how bad he was hurting his family with his decease, I tried a couple of years ago to help him, I flue out to see him around 2 years ago and I couldn't help him, and I wanted so much to help my brother, they are not living in a good place, a flop house I guess that's what they call it, but the good news is he at least excepted that he was an alcoholic, and I told him that was a start and that now he needed to go get help, But another tragedy came and I lost my grandma, so of course I came back right away and went to my dear grandmas funeral. And now this loosing a brother or anyone who is so close to you is so hard. I am beside myself, I don't want to go into work today, matter of fact I heaven even told my boss that I lost my brother, I never realized how hard it would be to get through something like this, and will I, can I only You dear Lord know how am I going to cope this day, I need to work to pay the bills, and have a good life, But now I am stuck in a muddy pit and I don't know if I can keep it together, Lord help us all, for those that maybe going through a very difficult time and just have lost someone dear, I can say I know how you feel, Its happening to me right now, the loss of someone so dear is truly a painful thing to go through with, its so darn hard, I want to make the right decisions and do the right things, but this happens Its like my world is crushing down on me and I don't want to loose it, I need to keep it together. R.I.P my big bro I will forever keep all the good times in my heart and I will try to remember all the fun times we had together growing up. And I am the one who keeps it together. Not now I know it takes time to heal from loosing anyone close to you, but this really hit home... See ya later, catch you on the flip side, I am going through a tough time right now and I want to do the right things, But I am struggling so much, for now, And I don't know how long the suffering will be, I feel like I can't deal with everything, But I know in my heart that *I* have Great, awesome, most wonderful God, mighty hand he is watching over me and helping me through this tragedy> I will make it through Because I have a great and wonderful, God who gives me peace BEYOUND my understanding, I feel like HE is my protector, My all, really, I need Jesus, once you find that peace, you will understand how it is so important to Liston to your parents and go back and study the Word, its all in there, the Ten commandments, and the laws set out in your home, Now I wont ever say stay if you feel like your parents don't understand, they DO...Know if ands or butts... saying well my parents may not understand, ask them to help you, turning to drugs and booze bear...

What ever your dreams are don't give up. what your going through But If you keep the percents out in the cold say, then they will fight you tooth and nail, They love you, with all there hearts and gave birth to you, they gave you life and God wanted you here for a reason...And don't lie and do everything you have done, Parents know they have such a loving hearts, they just didn't know how to parent you, they had there own difficulty's to deal with I am sure there where many.

PS.

Now go and live life, learn like we all do and need to do. My life will forever been like in the wind, sweetly softly blowing.

Lord God I pray that this book will help one, even just one, then I know my job is done. Lord please help me to continue to forgive myself for all the wrong, for all the hurt, for all the pain that I have caused, for the pain I have caused my family and to all my friends. I hold dear. I will forever be grateful for the lessons I have learned along the way. I will be in debt to my Lord and I will be finally free.

Like a bird when it has to leave the nest, I am that bird I am going to spread my wings and fly, like an Eagle...

Dear God:

Today I start counselling and I am looking forward to talking to someone about my issues. Sometimes I wish I could just get help and be healed of my mental illness that I wouldn't have to suffer any more. I want to go all natural and be healthy. I get headaches and sickness and constipation. Form the pills the doctors give me. Like who likes that. So I want to check out fiddle-heads; I hear it is a great place to go and get natural herbal remedies.

I want to continue to help as many lost souls. I want to live my life to the fullest, I plan on travailing the world promoting my books and helping the lost, I know that's why I am here on this earth.

There is so much I can teach, I have a wonderful Teacher his name is Jesus, and he helps me all the time, he is a trusted friend, and only wants whats best for us, we are the ones who get our self in trouble. If we could just listen and not go astray. Life would be good all the time, yes headache's come and we can get hurt, but God is the one we should run to when in trouble. I will look forward to all your response and how you feel about my books. When the Lord promises you something; He will do it, you just need to obey Him and do what He wants you to do, He will be by your side forever.

He said, he will never leave us or forsake us. So; I trust him with my whole life, everything I am, and I know He will guide me until its my time to go from this earth.

You should get your bible, if you don't have one there are churches/Library that you can borrow from. So you can refer to it as you read my books.

Zecharíah 7, 8

It says in **verse 7:10** Do not oppress the widow or the fatherless, the alien or the poor. In your hearts do not think evil of each other.

8:3 This is what the lord says: "I will return to Zion and dwell in Jerusalem. Then Jerusalem will be called the city of truth, and the mountain of the Lord almighty will be called the "Holy Mountain"

8:7 I will save my people from the countries of the east and the west. I will bring them back to live in Jerusalem; they will be my people, and I will be faithful and righteous to them as their God.

See God tells us these things and we are to pay attention, we need to follow God or we will get lost again.

8:16 These are the things you are to do: Speak the truth to each other, and render truth and sound judgment in your courts; do not plot evil against your neighbor, and do not love to swear falsely. I hate all this declares the Lord almighty.

So we should Liston to God and try our best to follow his commandments. By for now talk again soon. Till then God bless...

Zechariah 12: 1

The Lord who stretches out the heavens, who lays the foundation of the earth, who forms the spirit of man within him, declares: I am going to make Jerusalem a cup that sends all the surrounding people reeling.

Verse 14: 20

On that day Holy to the Lord will be inscribed on the bells of the horses, and the cooking pots in the Lords house will be like the sacrifice bowls in front of the alter. Every pot in Jerusalem and Judah will be Holy to the Lord Almighty, and all who come to sacrifice will take some of the pots and cook in them. And on that day there will no longer be a Canaanite in the house of the Lord Almighty.

My Prayer:

Thank you Lord for your word, I know sometimes we don't understand it, and times we are confused, but if we stand in your name, we will keep trying to understand and do your will. I thank you Lord for helping me understand, thank you for never giving up on me, thank you for your great and loving arms, I want to serve you Lord God forever. Amen

There are times in your life that you want to give up, don't. There is so much more to life then what your going through. Lean on Him who understands what your going through. He will help; just ask and then wait, in time you will see Him move, and He will do it, just wait on the Lord God Almighty.

I admit that I have not had the patience to wait, and got myself in a whole lot of mess, so please here me when I say "wait on the Lord", he will come through for you, if that's His will, because our wills are different then His and he knows what we need before we even ask. I will be kind to all the people I meet.

I will do my best and my best will do. Amen

And if I make a mistake again, and mess up I know God understands, he is the one who made me, gave me to my mom, and she loves me dearly, I just want you all to understand, life is hard;, I think when we go through trials and we have trouble we have to look at our choices, are we following our own desires or are we following Gods plan...

"Gods plan you ask"?, If we look inside the great and awesome Book " Called the Bible" we will find the answers, they are there and if we need guidance we should ask the elders of the Church. Do your research on Bible apps, and keep asking and never give up on your dreams. "God is good, all the time".

I am still in the shelter, its been 2 months and 3 weeks, give or take a day; Its been rough I have to say, I am still reading the bible and doing, things for people. Like helping them in any way I can, I love to help people, I get a lot of satisfaction helping others, It makes me feel good knowing I can help; even in my pain. And talking to God, the Holy Spirit and Jesus, I feel good, he makes me feel better and loved. There is know other Love then from the Father. Thank you Father God, thank you Jesus and thank you Oh Holy Spirit.

I love to Liston to Music, it soothes my soul, especially Christian music, I think God speaks to me through music, and it makes me feel so loved. So excepted, I do feel special because I am His and know one can snatch me out of His loving arms. Know one, not even the evil one. I am Gods and I want to keep moving up and beyond my past, I will take what I've learned and use it to help others. I can with God as my Guide and helper in ever present time.

I am in a better place today then last week, but my emotions go up and down here. Its not easy staying at a shelter, with all woman, get a whole bunch of woman together, (that have been abused in some form), well you know what happens! Craziness, But the strong will survive we can help each other, its just that some people have a hard time expressing there feelings, and that's

OK for now. In do time when your ready then you can release the pain. Going to get help makes you a better person. It helps and I am living prove, why not get the help. They want to help us, and there are so many resources out there. Reach out... Reach up and keep looking forward. Don't give up... Till later, have a great day and or night and remember, someone out there in this world; Loves you!

God Bless

Psalm 82-3

Defend the cause of the weak and fatherless; maintain the rights of the poor and oppressed. Rescue the weak and the needy; deliver them from the hands of the wicked.

Psalm 83-1, 17,18

O God do not keep silent; be not quiet, O God, be not still.

May they ever be ashamed and dismayed; may they parish in disgrace. Let them know that you, whose name is the Lord-- that you alone are the most high over all the earth.

I am going through the Psalm and I am finding it very interesting, I have went through them before, but I didn't get it all. I am now learning more about David and his life. By the way my brothers name is David, so I can talk to my brother and help him understand God through the book of David, its interesting to know that there are lots of names out there who have biblical names, I never gave my daughters biblical names, but I definitely ask God for my second daughters name, I didn't know what to name her, so I prayed and her name came to me. Cool aye. Back to David, he was a strong man, a man with few words, sounds like my brother, a strong man; He became king, and did some amazing things for God. He made mistakes, and paid the price, so you see we all have our faults, but God can fix us or use us, He can do all things. I believe, wont you?

Today, I am going to get things done, I am glad I started to write in my book again, I really do enjoy writing, it s fun and I always feel better after. Lord show me the way today, if someone needs some kind words, let them flow form my lips to them, help me comfort them, for you alone know what they need. Amen

Thank you Lord God for always being there for me. Thank you for your loving kindness, your power and your might. God bless this place, and please go before me, amen.

Psalm 84: 1,2- 10,12

How lovely is your dwelling place, O Lord almighty?
My soil yearns even faints, for the courts of the Lord; my heart and my flesh cry out for the living God. Better is one day in your courts then a thousand elsewhere; I would rather be a doorkeeper in the house of my God then dwell in the tents of the wicked. O Lord Almighty blessed is the man who trust in you.

I am still reading Psalm and I am finding it to be interesting, some times I don't understand why things happen, or didn't happen, But I have a God who is understanding, and can help me understand. I can keep learning, even though I have a learning advisability, It doesn't define me. Dave had a disability and that didn't stop him, when God said I want you David, he just asked for help, and even though God new him every part of him, (and God new in his great wisdom) that David would ask for the help, he just needed to get the courage and wisdom from God. Sometimes we think we can do it on our own, but for me, I know I need Jesus, he is the only way for me, He is the only one who knows my limits. As for me I will serve the Lord for the rest of my life.

When I face challenges I know who to turn to. I also believe God brings people in our lives to help us grow, and to teach us. We are all teachers in a way, if we have kids we are teaching them all the time, and if we keep an open mind, we can be taught so much, I believe we can help each other and our self, if we would not be so stubborn.

We need to Liston more with ears; I mean that's why God gave us 2 ears and only one mouth. Talk less, Liston more.

This is a hard lesson to learn when your so caught up in your self, I didn't think I was once, and it got me in a whole lot of trouble, even though I thought I was doing it right; I learned that I need to get out of my own way sometimes. If you understand what that means. I didn't at first understand, but someone explained it to me. And I have to keep watch and keep asking God to help me. I think learning is a life time thing. If we just get out of our own way and start listening more to the people who want only the best for us, then we will be better off. And it will be then, that we hear our God. May God bless you and may His face shine upon you and yours. Forever learning!

Psalm 86: 3, 4, 5, 11, 15

Have mercy on me, O Lord, for I call to you all daylong.
Bring Joy to your servant for to you O Lord. I lift up my soul.
You are forgiving and good, O Lord, abounding in love to all who call to you.

Teach me your way O Lord, and I will walk in your truth; give me an undivided heart, that I may fear your name.

But you O Lord are a compassionate and gracious God, slow to anger, abounding in love and faithfulness.

For you O Lord have helped me and comforted me.

Yes you have given me reason to live, reason to give, and hope beyond measure, you give me peace and I am grateful for your forgiveness, I am grateful you don't hold things against me like humans do. We are a strange kind.

Lord show us the way, keep us save and never let me go. I am yours Lord for ever, and ever.

Thank you Jesus for your gratefulness, for your great sacrifice for us, so we can be saved. I love you God. Amen

Morning prayers are always a good thing. I love to get up early with the birds and wild life, one day I hope I can live in the country and enjoy the nature every day.

Today I read from Psalm again, here is what I read.

Psalm 88: 1, 2 and 9

O Lord, the God who saves me, day and night I cry out before you. May my prayer come before you; turn your ear to my cry. I am confined and cannot escape; my eyes are dim with grief. I call to you, O Lord, every day; I spread out my hands to you.

Thank you Lord God for your word, I am grateful you have given us this great book to read, to reflect and grow with. I am hoping the next 50 years of my life is better then the last 50. I want to go exploring and learn more about Canada, its a great big world out there, so many places to see and do. My hope is I have friends to do it with. I just want to explore so many places, I hope I can do it. If its the Lords will, I can because I can do all things through Him who gives me strength. Thank you Lord for giving me another day to help others. Amen

---

Psalm 89: 1, 2, 7, 8, 11, 15, 16

I will sing of the Lords great love forever; with my mouth I will make your faithfulness through all generations.2. I will declare that your love stands firm forever, that you established your faithfulness in heaven its self.

7, 8 In the council of the holy ones God is greatly feared;

He is more awesome then all who surround him. O Lord God Almighty who is like you? You are mighty, O Lord and your faithfulness surrounds you.11.The heavens are yours, and yours also the world and all that is in it.

Verse's 15,16 Blessed are those who learn acclaim you, who walk in the light of your presence, O Lord. They rejoice in your name all day long; they exult in your righteousness.

My prayer:

Thank you Lord God for your word, your great book of knowledge, without it I would be lost, as I was before. But I am found and I never want to loose myself again, this is why your book is so good to us, it helps us learn and grow.

I am forever grateful and I always will be. I cant live with out your Love and I am so glad you found me. Amen

---

Psalm 90: 2, 10, 15, 16, 17

Before the Mountains were born or you brought forth the earth and the world, from everlasting to everlasting you are God.

The length of our days is seventy years—or eighty, if we have the strength; yet their span is but trouble and sorrow, for they quickly pass, and we fly away.

Make us glad for as many days as you have afflicted us, for as many years as we have seen trouble. May your deeds be shown to your servants, your splendour to their children.

May the favor of the Lord our God rest upon us; establish the work of our hands for us—yes, establish the work of our hands. Amen

Thank you Lord God for your work here on earth, may we take care of it daily, may we feel your love always. Lord show me the way and I will go. Amen

---

Psalm 91: 1, 2, 7, 8, 14, 15, 16

As you read this reflect on what is said. Maybe study this one for a month, and reflect on what Jesus is saying and how much He truly does want the best for us.

He who dwells in the shelter of the Most High will rest in the shadows of the Almighty. I will say of the Lord, "He is my refuge and my fortress, my God, in whom I trust".

A thousand may fall at your side, ten thousand at your right hand, but it will not come near you. You will only observe with your eyes and see the punishment of the wicked.

Because He loves me, "says the Lord," I will rescue him; I will protect him, for he acknowledges my name.

He will call upon me, and I will answer him; I will be with him in trouble, with long life will I satisfy him and show him my salvation"

Thank you Lord God for your mighty hand, for the protection over us, for showing me your ways through the Bible, teach me and I will follow, I want to serve you O Lord for the rest of my life, I will say it again, for the rest of my life. As long as I have you I have nothing to fear. Even when people try to hurt me, you will give me a shield with witch to use to protect me from the arrows that come my way. I want to serve you only and I am happy to do this. Amen

---

Psalm 92: 4, 5, 9, 15

For you make me glad by your deeds, O Lord: I sing for joy at the works of your hands. How great are your works O Lord, how profound your thoughts!

For surely your enemies, O Lord surely your enemies will parish; and evildoers will be scattered.

"The Lord is upright; he is my Rock, and there is no wickedness in him."

Psalm 93: 3, 4.

The seas have lifted up, O Lord the seas have lifted up their voice; the seas have lifted up their pounding waves. Mightier then the thunder of the great waters, mightier then the breakers of the sea-- The Lord on high is mighty.

Thank you Lord God for your mighty hands. Lord God please go before me and make a way, where there seems to be no way. Thank you Jesus for your sacrifice; yourself so we can be saved. Amen

May God bless you today.

Psalm 94: 3, 4, 5, 6, 8, 10, 12, 23

How long will the wicked, O Lord how will the wicked be jubilant? They crush your people, O Lord; they oppress your inheritance. They slay the widow and the alien; they murder the fatherless.

Take heed, you senseless ones among the people; you fools when will you become wise? Does He who planted the ear not hear? Does He who formed the eye not see? Does He who disciplines nations not punish?

Blessed is the man you discipline, O Lord, the man you teach from your law; you grant him relief from the days of trouble, till a pit is dug for the wicked.

For the Lord will reject His people; he will never forsake His inheritance.

When anxiety was great within me, your consolation brought joy to my soul.

But the Lord has become my fortress, my God the Rock in whom I take refuge. He will repay them for their wickedness; the Lord our God will destroy them.

Thank you Lord God for your word, I am grateful I have become one of your chosen ones, thank you Lord God, I am so great-full. Please Lord give me travailing mercy's as I drive out to see my sister, In Toronto. Help me be the light to her soul, and help me speak the words to her, to help her come back to you. She is a lost soul wondering and not sure where to go, please give her peace and Joy as the only way you can. I know she will find her way back, please help me help her. Amen

I am at my sisters in Toronto this weekend.

Reading Psalm still, I am trying to understand the writer David and how God has helped him in his troubles.

Psalm 95

I am not going to write it all out, but I think it would be good to read it all. And study this one.

Come, let u sing for joy to the Lord; let us shout aloud to the Rock of salvation. Let us come before him with thanksgiving and extol him with music and song.

For the Lord is the great God, the great King above all gods.

Verse 6 come let us bow down in worship, let us kneel before the Lord our Maker. For he is our God and we are the people of his pasture, the flock under his care.

I love the psalm, for several reasons, one being its my brother Dave's name, and I have gone through some very difficult times in my life, and the psalm was a place to feel refreshed, renewed and it is always good for the soul, as you continue on your faith Journey, keep reading the book of Psalm it is very comforting and you will begin to love it. And David to.

May God bless you on your walk of faith. Don't ever give up, I wont. God bless

P.S. As you read Davids songs and reflect on your own life, may you find peace and joy in your personal faith journey.

God bless you as you do.

Psalm 97: 7, 9, 10, 12

All who worship images are put to shame, those who boast in idols-worship him, all you gods..

For you, O Lord are the most high over all the earth; you are exalted far above all gods.

Let those who love the Lord hate evil, for he guards the lives of his faithful ones and delivers them from the hand of the wicked. Rejoice in the Lord, you who are righteous, and praise his Holy name.

Thank you Lord God for your word, please go before me and give me travailing mercy's and shine your light for those to see your glory, may I be a shinning light to the lost, may I be kind and loving to all who speak to me. Lord God I pray I would be loving and kind always. Amen

---

Psalm 98: 3, 7, 8, 9

He has remembered his love and his faithfulness to the house of Israel; all the ends of the earth have seen the salvation of our God. Let the sea resound, and everything in it, the world and all who live in it. Let the rivers clap their hands, let the mountains sing for joy; let them sing before the Lord, for he comes to judge the world in righteousness and the people with equity.

Psalm 99: 2,3,5,7

Great is the Lord in Zion; he is exalted over all the nations. Let them praise your great and awesome name- He is holy.

Exalt the Lord our God and worship at his footstool, he is Holy. They called on the Lord and He answered them. He spoke to them form a pillar of cloud; they kept his statutes and the decrees they gave them.

Thank you Lord God for your word, for watching over us through the night. I love you Lord God with all my heart, may I be a faithful servant forever, may I be a voice for you when their lost and need guidance. Lord please give me peace and take away all the pain, Lord please heal me of my mental illness, help me be well again, Lord you said ask and we will receive; please heal me of my mental illness, show me the way O Lord. I want to do whats right and just, I want to be a good servant, I want to follow you all the days of my life.

Lord please help the lost, please give to the less fortunate, my hope is if I ever win any money, to give to the less fortunate I want to build wells and give to the needy, Lord please provide for the ones on the streets. Please here my prayers, Amen

We read in Job, and how everything was taken from him. In **verse 32**, he is talking to three men. This is what a young one has said.

"I am young in years, and you are old; that is why I was fearful, not daring to tell you what I know. I thought age should speak; advanced years should teach wisdom! But it is the spirit in a man, the breath of the almighty, that gives him understanding.

Job has lost everything, and he is trying to understand why, why has God allowed it, he soon will find out as God is going to reveal it to him and let him know; He will restore him; Job will be king gain one day, and he will see the glory of God one day when he leaves this world.

I believe God has a plan for all of us, we just need to step aside and let Him work in our lives.

I am living in my new place now, still in Kitchener, but I know one day I may move from here, I don't know. But for now I will continue to write and live and love, I will do my best and let God do the rest, He will be there for you and I, we just have to keep the faith.

I believe God is working things out for me, I just need to be patient and learn to wait for the Lord, I will do my best and keep moving, keep living and I will be the best that I can be.

Lord please be with us forever more, Lord show me the way I should go, teach and help me I pray; Help my family Lord, help them be closer to you, to be reading your word every day, and not give up hope in their dreams, May we always know you Lord and walk with you daily. Please help my girls in their walk with you Lord, show them the way. Help them when they are lost and please Lord I pray they never go astray. Lord here my prayers. Amen God is good!

God is speaking to Job and this is what he said:

Job 33: 4, 26

The spirit of God has made me; the breath of the Almighty gives me life.

He prays to God and finds favour with him. He sees Gods face and shouts for joy; he is restored by God to his righteous state.

Then he went to men and said he had sinned and was not right, but that God restored him and made him whole again. I believe we can be restored and I want to hear Gods voice, I want to know I am doing the right things, and making the right decisions, Lord show me the way, and help me I pray.

Lord you know my dreams, please help me to achieve them, Lord help me to be kind, and to help when I can, I want to be free of fear and be open and honest. I want to do whats right.

Lord please help me. Thank you for watching over us and keeping us safe. Lord I love you and want to serve you. Amen

P.S. I am leaving to Alberta on Friday, cant wait to spend some time with my dad, it is going to be interesting, and I hope we have fun, I found him last year, Lord be with us and help us, Amen

Reading in Job still and having a hard time with some of it. I am struggling with the fact that God allowed Satan to take away all his family and all his possessions. It doesn't make sense to me sometimes, I don't understand everything in the bible and why things happy, I do know the world is evil and there are forces out there that are beyond our understanding,

SO I will keep looking to the bible to help me understand, I hope one day I find a good partner with whom I can study with, and become more knowledgeable of the bible and what God is doing. I want to keep growing in my faith and I hope you do to. Life's a journey lets make it a good one.

So I leave Friday to go see my father, (I talked about him in my first book) and I am so excited to have this time with him, I will also get to meet my half sister, I am so happy. I have so much to look forward to, I just hope I can keep making enough money to go out to see all my family, I want to get to know them more and learn more about my history. Life is good, I just have to take one day at a time, as I do suffer with depression so I struggle, But I know there is better up ahead, I just need to keep looking up and not back, Lord show me how. Amen

Lord thank you for your word, it is sweet to my lips, and warms my heart, Thank you Jesus.

I am reading Song Of Songs

Verse 2:16

Beloved:

My lover is mine and I am his; he browses among the lilies.

Until the day breaks and the shadows flee, turn, my lover, and be like a gazelle or like a young stag on the rugged hills.

Verse 3: 9,10

King Solomon made for himself the carriage; he made it of wood from Lebanon. Its posts he made of silver, its base of gold. Its seat was upholstered with purple, its interior lovingly inlaid by the daughter of Jerusalem.

I thank you Lord for your word and for showing us your plans, help me in my unbelief, show me the way I should go and guide my hands, Amen

---

Song of Songs 4: 1, 7, 9, 10

How beautiful you are, my darling! Oh, how beautiful!

Your eyes behind your veil are doves. Your hair is like a flock of goats descending from mount Gilead.

All beautiful you are my darling there is know flaw in you.

You have stolen my heart, my sister my bride, you have stolen my heart with one glance of your eyes, with one jewel of your necklace. How delightful is your love, my sister, my bride!

How much more pleasing is your love then wine, and the fragrance of your perfume then any spice!

In this passage I believe he is calling her sister as in Christ sister, not blood sister, I think its a figure of speech, not really his sister per say, its confusing for someone new to their faith, So I thought I would explain it better to you who don't understand. It is only through Jesus blood when we become sisters and brothers in Christ. Hopefully that helps you.

I am trying to figure out if I should work in the hospital, or continue to do home care, I have to pray about this, as I am wanting a change, I need a change, and I need to make more money to pay my bills. Lord please help me make the right decisions, Lord I need you in all that I do. Lord please give us hope for today, and help us I pray. Amen

Today is a bit cold outside, I awoke early this am, I was thinking about things I need to get and what I want to do. I would love to buy some land and live off the grid, that would be nice, especially if I had help, like from my brother and kids they cold live there to. We could be happy, I would build a big green house and put all my veggies on tables so I wouldn't have to bend. And I would grow so much stuff, we could be very happy with all the fresh veggies, and I would have fruit trees lots of fruit trees for the grandkids to pick and eat. It would be so nice, maybe it will happen one day, I would need lots of money to start this, as I would be starting from the ground up. I love to dream, I would want a good strong man to help me to. I strong Christian man, someone who is strong in his faith with the Lord, he would except me and love me just the way I am. I could finally get a horse and some chickens, and other animals, we could have a hobby farm and bring out people to our farm, we could have party's and enjoy each others company. That would be very nice. And I would be very happy...

Off to work, I go. Have a wonderful day or night!

God bless

Today is raining outside, more of a drizzle then anything, I awoke early this am, didn't want to but that's the way it goes.

Song Of Songs 6:1, 7:1

Verse 6:1 Where has your lover gone, most beautiful of woman? Which way did your lover turn, that we may look for him with you?

Verse 7:1 Your graceful legs are like jewels, the work of a craftsman's hands.

Beloved; May the wine go straight to my lover, flowing gently over lips and teeth. I belong to my lover, and his desire is for me. Come, my lover, let us go to the countryside, let us spend the night in the villages.

I think what Solomon's is saying and trying to tell us is he has a lover and she is most beautiful and he admires her, she is his Queen, I think Solomon is a very good man, he loves his wife and treats her well. I hope I can say that one day, that I meet a man and he treats me well, and respects me, I know he's out there, just haven't met him yet. SO I will keep dreaming and keep working towards a better life. I am a good person and I believe, I can do all things through Christ who strengthens me. Thank you Jesus, for your care over me and my family. Thank you Jesus for your awesomeness.

I am blessed, I am loved and I am taken care of.

God bless you and yours.

Song Of Songs 8:2

I would lead you and bring you to my mothers house- She who has taught me. I would give you spice wine to drink, the nectar of my pomegranates. His left arm is under my head and his right arm embraces me. Daughters of Jerusalem, I charge you: Do not arouse or awaken love until it so desires.

V13 “Lover” You who dwell in the gardens with friends in attendance, let me hear your voice!

V14 “Beloved” Come away my lover, and be like a gazelle or like a young stag on the spice-laden mountains.

Wow I think these verses are very raw, but that’s how some of the text is written, I don’t always understand it but I know it was God breathed So if its Gods word I must try to understand it; Lord help me understand your word, and learn from its pages, I am like a little child who is looking up to the almighty, and I need guidance Lord show me the way, I do not want to turn right or left Just straight to your loving arms I go.

Thank you Lord God for watching over us and keeping us safe, thank you that I live in a free country, I am So glad to be Canadian. Amen

Today I have a long day I work till 4:30 but its not to bad, I will be driving half the time. Picking up someone from the hospital to bring them home.

Jeremiah 32:33

They turned their backs to me and not their faces; though I taught them again and again, they would not listen or respond to discipline.

They wear setting up their abominable Idols, to worship and the Lord God was not happy with this, So God has sent them a massage He will sent plagues and famine and so much more them they will ever see, God has a Anger you don't want to stir So I think some people don't know Him that well, as for them to think they could do that and not be punished. They are not in their right minds, they have lost it. Its hard to believe they would turn from God for he saved them and gave them land, If I was given land I would not turn from God how could I when he just blessed me. It doesn't make sense, so they must of been out of their minds. That's all I can figure.

In Verse 33, we see God has forgiven them and wants to bless them again, if they would turn from their wickedness. He promise's them restoration of the land, He wants to bless them. God is good and forgives us, if we would only just trust to him fully and lean on Him who knows all and understands all. We would be better off. Lord show me the way, teach me your laws and help me I pray, Amen

I read a few passages in the bible this am, but I am not going to write about it now, as I believe I have other things I need to say, I hope the Lord can speak through me to you and help you on your faith Journey; I believe that God speaks to us all the time, we just need to sit back and listen and turn all devices off, and just listen, he will speak if we ask him to help us and give Him the opportunity to talk to you. We all come form our mother and we all have a desire to be loved and to love but we choose to fight, "why cant we all just get along", we say, but we have to be the ones to start, if they don't we must, so give it a try, say a kind word or give someone a hug, you will feel better and so will they. Life is hard, some of us feel as though we have been given a bad life, but its our own choices that determine where we are going and what we will be doing in this life, we are the ones who make the decisions to listen or go our own way. We have tried our way lets try Gods way now. So just say one pray "Lord help me" and He will be there, God said just call out my name and I will help you. Trust Him; he has your best interest at heart. I have your best interest at heart. Don't give up or give into this crazy world. Just trust Him who knows all about you, Yes even those not so nice parts, and He still loves you. What do you have to loose. Life will get better, and If you trust the Lord He will help you. I believe that.

Lord please take away the unbelief in these people whom you love and want to care for. Amen

---

Lamentations 3: 22-27, 39-42, 55-59, 61,62 3: 22-42

Because of the Lords great love we are not consumed, for his compassion's never fail. They are new every morning; great is your faithfulness. I say to myself, "The Lord is my portion; therefore I will wait for Him". The Lord is good to those who's hope is in him," it is good to wait quietly for the salvation of the Lord. It is good for a man to bear the yoke while he is young.

Question: Why should any living man complain when punished for his sins? Let us examine our ways and test them, and let us return to the Lord, let us lift our hearts and our hands to God in heaven, and say; we have sinned and rebelled and you have forgiven us. Amen

Verse 55-63

I called on your name, oh Lord, from the depths of the pit. You heard my plea: "Do not close your ears to my cry for relief"

You came near when I called you, and you said "do not fear"

You have seen, oh Lord, the wrong done to me. Uphold my cause.

Oh Lord you have heard their insults, all their plots against me- what my enemies whisper and mutter against me all day long.

This is my Prayer;

This is how we feel sometimes, that we wish the Lord would heal us, fix us, hear our cry's, He does, we just need to be patient, and that can be very hard at times. I often wonder why does it takes so long, I only wish for good for all my family even my enemies. I Just hope Lord you can help me, financially I am struggling, I can hardly make mends meet, know money for food for the next 2 weeks. Lord please help us. Amen

I was reading in **Ezekiel 1,2,3**

Not all of it, I was scanning through. I find it hard to concentrate as there is a lot of killing and wars, and slaughterer, So it is disturbing. And that's why I don't recommend it for new Christian's, as it is hard to read and to understand, just to think about it sometimes it bothers me, I don't understand it, and thats why I think it bothers me so. I have to stop reading if it bothers me and Jesus understands how I feel. That's what I am so happy about; that He truly does understand what we're going through and how we feel. I am so grateful that I have a God who understands me and is patient with me. He never pushes me beyond what I can handle, and I know he helps me through it, I just have to rely on Him more. I trust him with my life, and I know He has my best at heart, I am just a human after all, and I make mistakes and I sometimes don't listen, but I try my best and that's what matters most, I did try and I leaned on Him who has my best at heart. Thank you Jesus for loving me for understanding me and for teaching me, show me the way and I will go, I want to do your will even though my will sometimes takes over. Lord help me to listen and obey. Amen

Reading in Daniel today;

Daniel 10: 1-19 12:,9,10

Now I have come to explain to you what will happen to your people, for the vision concerns a time yet to come" While he was saying this to me, I bowed with my face to the ground and was speechless. Then one who looked like a man touched my lips and I opened my mouth and began to speak. I said to the one before me, "I am overcome with anguish because of the vision , my Lord and I am helpless. How can I, your servant, talk with you, my Lord? My strength is gone and I can hardly breathe". Again the one who look like a man touched me and gave me strength. Do not be afraid, O man highly esteemed," he said ''Peace! Be strong now; be strong"

When he spoke to meI was strengthened and said "speak, my Lord, since you have given me strength."

Verse 12: 9,10

He replied, "Go your way, Daniel, because the words are closed up and sealed until the time of end. Many will be purified, made spotless and refined, but the wicked will continue to be wicked.

None of the wicked will understand, but those who are wise will understand.

Thank you for your word Lord, please go before me and make a way, Lord I am yours now and forever more. Amen

---

Daniel 12: 1-4, 9,10 and 13

At that time Michael, the great prince who protects your people will arise. There will be a time of distress such as has not happened from the beginning of nations until then. But at that time your people- everyone whose name is found written in the book- will be delivered. Multitudes who sleep in the dust of the earth will awake: some to everlasting life, others to shame and everlasting contempt. Those who are wise will shine like the brightness of heavens, and those who lead many to righteousness, like the starts for ever and ever. But you Daniel, close up and seal the words of the scroll untill the time of the end. Many will go here and there to increase knowledge.

Verse 9

he replied, "Go your way, Daniel because the words are closed up and sealed until the time of the end. Many will be purified, made spotless and refined, but the wicked will continue to be wicked. None of the wicked will understand, but those who are wise will understand.

Verse 13

As for you, go your way till the end. You will rest, and then at the end of the days you will rise to receive your allotted inheritance.

Thank you Jesus. Lord you are my only hope, I have found. And I don't want to loose it again, thank you Lord for giving me hope, and for always being there for me. I love you Lord God and I want to serve you and live for you. You give me peace and I feel the love, thank you Jesus, Amen

I read in Hosea this morning, but I find the old chapters are hard to understand, and this one I am having a hard time with, I often wonder why all the blood shed, why all the wars, why cant people just get along, why do we fight? I know that for most fights its for your right, but to kill someone for it, its crazy, I will ask the Lord to help me understand it, because there are reasons for it all to be put in the bible right. I mean God wanted us to read it and understand it, so I will read it but not before I ask God to help me understand it. As I find it disturbing to say the least, but I do have depression and when you have mental illness it makes it even harder to understand. I don't want to discourage you, but just to tell you it is difficult to understand So please pray and ask God to help you understand it and reveal its meaning behind it, and to study it from your heart, as it was written in a time of many great battles. I just hope your faith journey keeps getting better and with more understanding of His word you will grow more spiritually.

Lord go before me and make a way, show me the way and teach me I pray, Lord open my mouth with your praises. May I be a good example to the people that are lost in their sin, may I be a loving person to all. Amen

---

Hosea 3:1-5

Hosea's Reconciliation with his wife:

The Lord said to me, "Go, show your love to your wife again, though she is loved by another and is an adulteress. Love her as the Lord loves the Israelite's, though they turn to other gods and love the sacred raisin cakes". So I bought her with Fifteen shekels of silver and about homer and lethek of barley. Then I told her, "You are to live with me many days; you must not be a prostitute or be intimate with any man, and I will live with you". For the Israelite will live many days without king or prince, without sacrifice or sacred stones, without ephod or idol. After the Israelite's will return and seek the Lord their God and David their King. They will come trembling to the Lord and to his blessings in the last days.

Well the old testament is hard to understand, I trying to do my best. I know we have to read the old testaments and learn from them, but boy is it hard to understand sometimes, I just don't like all the killings and evil that is written in there. I will keep asking God to help me through it. Lord show me the way, teach me your will and help me I pray. Amen

I was reading Obadiah, Its a short book. You could read it in 5 minutes, its that's short, I didn't highlight anything because I wasn't sure what to say about it.

I am a little upset today, wishing I could get the money together so I could publish my books, and I wonder if this is just my dream or is God going to help me do this? I am wondering because Its taking so long. I don't know, and I wonder if this is just something I want to do, and its not Gods will. I often wonder that, because its taking so long. Lord please help me to know without a doubt that you want me to publish these books, or not. Amen

I read in Jonah this am,

Jonahs prayer; verse 2

From inside the fish Jonah prayed to the Lord his God. He said. "In my distress I called to the Lord, and he answered me. From the depths of the grave I called for help, and you listened to my cry. You hurled me into the deep, into the very heart of the seas, and the currents swirled around me; all the waves and breakers swept over me, I said, I have been banished from your sight; yet I will look again toward your holy temple. The engulfing waters threatened me, the deep surrounded me; seaweed was wrapped around my head. But you brought my life up from the pit, O Lord my God.

What I have vowed I will make good. Salvation comes from the Lord." And the Lord commanded the fish, and it vomited Jonah onto dry land.

Jonahs book is something, first he is driven away then almost ship wrecked, then thrown out to sea then swallowed up by a fish, wow and he survived it all. Amazing, God is amazing.

So I guess we need to read the Good book and see our life is OK, we are OK. Life sometimes throws a curve ball; but if we stand firm with the help of our God we can make it through anything, we just need to trust the Lord. Amen

Thank you Lord for showing me I can get through it all, I just need to let go and trust you with everything. Amen

What do they say, another day another dollar?

I Am still reading from Jonah:

Jonah's Anger at the Lord's Compassion

But Jonah became greatly displeased and became angry. He prayed to the Lord, "O Lord, is this not what I said when I was still at home? This is why I was so quick to flee to Tarnish. I knew that you are gracious and compassionate God slow to anger and abounding in love, a God who relents from sending calamity . Now, O Lord, take away my life for it is better for me to die then to live." But the Lord replied, "Have you any right to be anger?"

Life isn't always the way we want it to be, it doesn't always seem fair, in our eyes or from our perspective, that is. But all is fair and just in Gods eyes. And we must resist the urge to doubt or judge like Jonah. Our part is to have faith and believe that God is just and all is in his control, weather or not we think, "Its just not fair".

I am glad I read Jonahs book, it has helped me realize I just have to rely on my God more and more each new day. Thank you Lord God, for all your love and care that you give each and everyone of us, we just need to reach out and ask. Amen

Thank you Jesus for showing me the way, please help me in my times of trouble and please give me peace. Amen

---

Matthew 17: 1-9

The Transfiguration; after six days Jesus took with him Peter, James and John the brother of James, and led them up on a high mountain by themselves. There he was transfigured before them. His face shone like the sun, and his clothes became as white as the light. Just then there appeared before them Moses and Elijah, talking with Jesus. Peter said to Jesus, "Lord it is good for us to be here. If you wish I will put up three shelters-one for you, one for Moses and one for Elijah". While he was still speaking, a bright cloud enveloped them, and a voice from the cloud said, "This is my son, whom I love; with him I am well pleased. Listen to him". When the disciples heard this, they fell face down to the ground, terrified. But Jesus came and touched them. "Get up" he said "Don't be afraid". When they looked up, they saw know one but Jesus. As they where coming down the mountain, Jesus instructed them, "Don't tell them what you have seen, until the son of Man has been raised from the dead." Thank you Jesus for watching over us and for answered prayers, I want to do your will, please help me do this. Amen

---

Matthew 18:1-7 16 and 19

At that time the disciples came to Jesus and asked, " Who is the greatest in the kingdom of heaven?". He called a little child and had him stand among them. And he said " I tell you the truth, unless you change and become like little children, you will never enter the kingdom of heaven. Therefore whoever humbles himself like this child is the greatest in the kingdom of heaven. And whoever welcomes a little child like this in my name welcomes me. But if anyone causes one of these little ones who believe in me to sin, it would be better for him to have a large millstone hung around his neck and to be drowned in the depths of the sea.

Verse 16

If your brother sins against you go and show him his fault, just between the two of you. If he listens to you, you have won your brother over. But if he will not listen, take one of two others along with you, so that every matter may be established by the testimony of two or three witnesses.

Again I tell you that if two of you on earth agree about anything you ask for, it will be done for you by the father in heaven. For where two or three come together in my name, there am I with them.

Lets pray Thank you Jesus for that reminder. I love you, please go before me and make a way, show me the way to go. And help me I pray. Amen

---

Matthew 25

The Parable of the Ten Virgins

'At that time the Kingdom of heaven will be like ten virgins who took their lamps and went out to meet the bridgroom. Five of them took their lamps and did not take any oil with them. The wise, however, took oil in jars along with their lamps. The bridegroom was a long time in coming, and they all became drowsy and fell asleep. "At midnight the cry came out: Here's the bridegroom come and meet him. Then all the virgins woke up and trimmed their lamps, the foolish ones said to the wise, give us some of your oil, our lamps are going out?" No' They replied, there may not be enough for both of us instead go to those who sell oil and buy some for yourselves. While they where on the way, the bridegroom came and the virgins went with him into the wedding banquet and the door was shut.

When the others came to the door, He did not open it to them, saying he doesn't know them. So the moral of the story, always be ready for Jesus, because he is coming one day. Be ready!

Gods calling each and everyone of us to a life of adventure. Remember an adventure is not an adventure unless there is some risk involved, are we willing to take some risks in our walk with Jesus. Are we willing to look a little foolish from time to time as we seek to develop new talents? If we are God will continue to bring us new opportunities of service. The warning of this parable is this; God holds us responsible for our lives and what we do with them.

The Joyful reward is this: One day we will stand before our God and hear Him say; Well done good and faithful servant". Matthew 25

I hope he says that to me, Lord please be with us today, show us the way. Amen

Reading in **Matthew 26**

The Lords Supper:

On the first day of the feast of the leavened bread, the disciples came to Jesus and asked, "where do you want us to make preparations for you to eat the Passover?" He replied, "Go into the city, to a certain man and tell him, my teacher says: My appointment time is near. I am going to celebrate the Passover with my disciples at your house. So the disciples did as Jesus had directed them and prepared the Passover.

At the Passover celebrations there was a disciple who was to betray Jesus, and most people know him as Judas, he was a man of faith but I think he lost it along the way, which is something that can and does happen to us all, we get lost. The most important thing is that we come back, we repent and move closer to God. We must keep our faith, we have to ask God to help us in our faith. Life gets hard sometimes and we tend to look to other resources, but Jesus is the truth and He will help us through this, He knows our weakness and can give us hope. I have struggled many times in my walk, but I keep going back and asking God to produce a good faith within me, and bring me back to where I belong, in his arms. Thank you Jesus for never giving up on me, thank you for bringing me back to you. I love you Lord God and I want to worship you all my days. Amen

You are a gift and Jesus is calling your name, come and He will give you rest, He will heal your wounds and bring good health back, trust Him who knows your all and everything about you, He has a plan for you. Keep looking to him.

Matthew 27: 11-14, 21-26

Jesus before Pilate

Now Peter just denied him 3 times, and was very upset with himself, he was outside crying, because he realized what Jesus had told him and it made him very unhappy.

Meanwhile Jesus stood before the governor, and the governor asked him, Are you the King of the Jews?"

"Yes, it is as you say," Jesus replied. When he is accused by the chief priests and elders, he gave no answer. Then Pilate asked him, "Don't you hear the testimony they are bringing against you?" But Jesus made know reply, not even to a single charge- to the great amazement of the governor.

So they went on to ask the crowd.

"Which of the two do you want me to release to you?" Asked the governor. "Barabbas", they answered. " What shall I do with Jesus who is called Christ?" Pilate asked, They all answered, Crucify him!" "Why what crime has he committed?" asked Pilate. But they shouted all the louder, "Crucify him". When Pilate seen he was getting no where, but that instead an uproar as starting, he took water and washed his hands in front of the crowd. "I am innocent of this mans blood," he said. "It is your responsibility!" All the people answered, "Let his blood be on us and our children!" Then he released Barabbas to them. But he had Jesus flogged, and handed over to be crucified.

Can you see it, the crowds and all the shouting, it would of been crazy, I would of been really sad, also, they new, the 12 new for sure, they were told by Jesus himself.

And to be a friend to Jesus, and to be able to touch him and feel his love; would of been so amazing. I know the times where hard and they went without, but we do even in this day an age, we go without or with less, I am just glad I gave my life to him who holds me dear. I am grateful for the tough times and for Him showing me the way out. I can be glad for I am a child of God. Thank you Jesus for saving me and giving me hope. Amen

---

Matthew 27: 50-53 28: 2

The death of Jesus

When Jesus cried out again in a loud voice, he gave up his spirit. At that moment the curtain of the temple was torn in two from top to bottom. The earth shook and the rocks split. The tombs broke open and bodies of many holy people who had died were raise to life. They came out of there tombs, and after Jesus resurrection they went into the holy city and appeared to many. The Guards at the tomb, after the Sabbath, there was an angle of the Lord came down from heaven and, going to the tomb, rolled back the stone and sat on it. His appearance was like lightning and his clothes were white as snow.

Can you imagination, How would you feel after seeing a angle? I would be like wow, they do look beautiful.

I cant even think about how people must of thought when Jesus didn't come down from the cross, you see He had a bigger plan. The people didn't understand everything. Jesus was going to change things, but he changed things from the moment He was thought of, He changed her soon to be husband in his mind, God spoke to him and helped him understand. I was glad He did. And He changed the world, He gave us understanding, hope and peace.

Thank you Jesus, for all that you do and all that you are. Please give me hope and peace, Lord please heal my mind and soul. Amen

---

Matthew 28:1-20

The Resurrection:

After the Sabbath, at dawn on the first day of the week, Mary Magdalene and the other Mary went to look at the tomb,. There was a violent earthquake, for an angel of the Lord came down from heaven and, going to the tomb, rolled back the stone and sat on it. His appearance was like lighting, and his clothes were white as snow. The guards were so afraid of him that they shook and became like dead men..

The angel said to the woman, " Do not be afraid, for I know that you are looking for Jesus, who was crucified. He is not here; he has risen, just as he said. Come and see the place where he lay. Then go quickly and tell his disciples: He has risen from the dead and is going ahead of you into Galilee. There you will see Him , Now I have told you."

You can get your bible and continue to read. I believe having your bible as a reference will help you in your faith Journey.

Today I woke up and was upset, I was thinking about all the people in the world and all the struggles we face, Its hard I know, I sometimes feel the weight of the world on my shoulders, but I know I have a great God who understands my feelings and what I am going through at that moment. He knows what I am thinking and how I am feeling.

I pray:

Lord please take away the stinking feelings I have and help me rest, I am also aware that God works everything out and that's why I am writing this now, I believe I was awakened by the Lord to write to you. I know my journey is not all that great, but I am still learning and growing and being, I am here and that's what matters. I can do all things through Christ who gives me strength. Ya I am going to mess up from time to time , we all do. But I can start over and begin again, I can be free from worry and fear; I shouldn't be afraid as I have someone who is more mighty then anyone I know. I am glad to have met Him and now I live my life for Him and he is all I got sometimes. He is my all.

My hope, my peace, my love. I want to share His love with you. May God richly bless you today. May you find your inner peace and may you sore like an eagle; high in the sky.

I will keep working till the day I die, weather it be volunteering or hard working, I will do my best and my best will do. And life will go on, we will survive this, this to will pass. This life will be good if only and only when I agree to keep the faith and not turn away from my Lord, I can do it one day at a time. There should be more groups out there for people who need it. I will continue to do my work here on earth... I am strong because God makes me strong. I am more then I even know, that I am... I am me and I will continue to ask God to help me love myself more. So much more that I see myself as He sees me. With know flaws. I can see me as he sees me only because I believe; I am a good person I want to be good and do good. This to comes from my God. I want to do good because He wants me to be good, I always want to do what my father tells me to do, and he helps me do it. I have 2 dads here on earth, and I want to make them both proud of me, But I want to please God more, so I liston as a child should. And I will continue to try and do good, and make my parents proud. But mostly I want to please my Lord God. I want to do his work and be a good soldier in this army of God.

I am so thankful for Google, I just have to ask her how to spell a word and she knows, I can ask her the weather; and she knows, its amazing. And all because of one person. who that is; I don't know but I am glad they made it., I am glad they decided to help us out and make such a thing as Google.

Thank you Google.

Okay I going to keep writing until I feel I need to stop, I will do whats right and be glad in it, I will be happy and be glad I have those feelings because those feeling I love to feel, I don't like feeling scared or intimated or fear. Its wearied though because I loved scaring people growing up, I was the one joking around and scaring people, like jumping out of a box or closet, my brothers taught me well, hahaha. Thanks Dave and Scott. You guys made my world. I am glad God gave me two brothers to hang out with. They tough me some not so good stuff to, but I tent to look at the good they brought to my life. unfortunately my brother Scott died of a bleeding ulcer 2 years ago, and it still hurts to talk about him, but I must. I will look back on all the good times we had, even though it was short lived. You see my brother Dave left for B.C. When I was a teen, and a few years later Scott went out. He has to be with his brother he missed him, meanwhile I am just starting my life as a mother and I was so busy with that that I didn't have much time with them in our adult years, So now I am trying to catch up. I will keep my brother's always in my prayers because their kinda like a wild child, just like I was. We have travelled a long way and life is not over yet. We have continue our relationship's just where we left off. I love my brother's both so much, Although I related more to Scott then Dave, probably the age difference I don't know, but I love them both, just differently. Now for my brother scoot his memory will be forever in my heart and I will cherish them, because that's all I got left from my brother Scott; just memories. Most of them great. I think my brother Scott started to have a good life out in B.C. He was with his brother, although I know it was a rocky one; they came through it alright. Brothers fight, its the forgiving that keeps us together. If we don't forgive, how can we expect to be forgiven. Right!, a hard truth but true. God is the one that helps us forgive; without His love and forgiveness how can we go on, just like robots or aliens I don't think so, we where made for more then that. We where made to be conquerors, worriers and fighters and we will fight for whats right. Even in times of trouble, we will fight the good fight. amen

Reading in Mark now. **Mark 1-8**

John the Baptist Prepares the Way:

It is written in Isaiah the prophet:

"I will send my messenger ahead of you, who will prepare the way" " a voice of one calling in the desert, Prepare the way for the Lord, make straight paths for Him." And so John came, baptizing in the desert region and preaching a baptism of repentance for the forgiveness of sin. The whole Judean countryside and all the people of Jerusalem went out to him. Confessing their sins, they were baptized by him in the Jordan River. John wore clothing made of camels hair, with a leather belt around his waist, and he ate locusts and wild honey. And this was his message: "After me will come one more powerful than I, the thongs of whose sandals I am not worthy to stoop down and untie. I baptize you with water, but He will baptize you with the Holy Spirit.

Yes, this was a man after Gods heart, he was a strong and a mighty man, someone who I think mattered to God and God helped him through all his struggles I am sure. I have to keep looking to the bible because it gives me hope, hope to keep going, even for just today. Even for one moment, I believe he wants us all to experience his great love and feel it in our hearts and souls. We are a loving kind not a hurtful kind. I always try to do my best and I know you will to, do what's right and you will be alright. That's sounds like a good name of a song. Ya "Do whats Right and you will be Alright, I might just sell that one. LoL

I am going in the direction of changing Jobs again. I loved being with kids, they make me smile, so I think I might do daycare again. I will pray and ask God; and if he sends some kids that will be great. Then I know this is my calling, but I am not sure right now. As I am older and, and I think; can I handle them wee ones again?. We will see.

Today I woke up thinking about my daughters, they are both Christian's and living the ways of the world. I am torn with this, I have to talk about this. They are 2 beautiful woman , my youngest has 2 boys, 13 and 10. I am concerned about their welfare. And I need to bring them to together and have a family meeting again. This time , I know will be a good thing and I know Jesus is making a way for me and them. And they want so much to get married. I hope that they Liston to me and understand it all. I believe this is going to change them, God is going to make a way. I wish for them to be happy, now I know we can do it on our own, and for some they should stay single. and I also know God created us for marriage.

To have children and to help each other. So my hope is they Liston and take what I have to say to heart. Lord please go before me and make a way. Amen

I am reading in **Mark 4: 26**

The Parable of the Growing Seed.

This is Jesus talking. He also said, " This is what the kingdom of God is like. A man scatters seed on the ground. Night and day, weather he sleeps or gets up, the seed sprouts and grows, though he does not know how. All by itself the soil produces grain- first the stalk, then the head, then the full kernel in the head. As soon as the grain is ripe, he puts a sickle to it, because the harvest has come.

What I get from this is He is the seed and He plants it in us, now we need to go out and plant the seeds in our family's and to our friends and everyone we meet. Jesus said go forth and produce, plant the seed.

That's it for today. Take care and do His work. Amen

Mark 5:1-20

I am not going to write it all out, but if you get your bible you can look at it and read it. This one was very hard to read and has been for a long time. Sometimes I avoid reading some passages because I don't always understand, and I am going through so much. But I will do my best.

So they went across the lake to the region of Gerasenes. When Jesus got out of the boat, a man with an evil spirit came from the tombs to meet him.

Now this man was living among the tombs know one could bind him any more, not even with chain. For he had often been chained hand and foot, but he tour the chains apart and broke the irons on his feet. No one was strong enough to subdue him. Night and day among the tombs and in the hills he would cry out and cut himself with stones. When he saw Jesus from a distance, he ran and fell on his knees in front of him. He shouted at the top of his voice, "what do you want with me, Jesus son of the most high God? Swear to God that you wont torture me!" For Jesus had said to him, " Come out of this man, you evil spirit" Then Jesus asked him, "what was his name?"

" My name is Legion," he replied, "for we are many,"

It must of been really scary for some to here this and read it, but God wants us to know how wonderful he is, how all powerful He is, how great and mighty Jesus is and the Lord wants us to be the best we can be, and do his work here on earth, for this is why we are here, for the lost to find Him. And when we find Jesus we should do good, turn away from bad, and follow Him who made us. I love you Lord God, please help me as I write and help me to speak and not be afraid to tell the truth, for the truth will set us free.

Lord please help us all who read this, understand you, help them and give them peace as they go about their duties. Lord show us the way to go, help us to be good people, help us to live your will not our own. For we have been bought with a price. And I thank you Jesus for coming to help us and save us from this wicked world in which we live.

Lord God: I want to be free form my issues, please help me get better and do your will better, and follow you till the end of time. Lord I need you and cant live without you. I thank you Jesus for the many talents you have given me, show me the way to go and

I will follow. Thank you God for giving us your son so we can be saved. Amen

---

Mark 6: 1-6

Jesus left there and went to his home town, accompanied by his disciples. When the Sabbath came, he began to teach in the synagogue, and many who heard him were amazed.

"Where did this man get these things?" they asked. "Whats this wisdom that has been given him, that he even does miracles!. Isnt this the carpenter? Isn't this Mary's son and brother of James, Joseph, Judas and Simon? Aren't his sisters here with us? And they took offence at him. Jesus said to them, " Only in his home-town, among his relatives and in his own house is a prophet without honor ." He could not do any miracles there, except lay his hands on a few sick people and heal them. And He was amazed at their lack of faith.

Faith: This is googles answer.

What is faith? When you have faith, you trust or believe in something very strongly. Some people have faith in a higher being, others put their faith behind the Red Sox. This noun comes from the old French word, meaning "Faith, belief, trust, confidence, pledge.

This is what we believe as Christians. Faith is being sure of what we hope for and certain of what we do not see.

So we know we have faith in something when we believe and trust that it is true. I believe God has a plan for us all and I know He can help you, as he has helped so many before us.

And I know in my heart this to be true. God can move that mountain just trust that he has your best interest at heart. He wants to help you, just have a little faith and He can move that mountain!. Amen

Thank you Jesus for showing me the way, for wanting me, and giving me that hope, and assurance that I don't have to worry about anything, I just have to turn to you, and know in my heart that I am making the right decisions. I can do this with all my strength and knowing you are with me I can succeed in my mission. I am a child of God and I can do all things through Jesus Christ who gives me that hope.

My prayer:

Lord you know this person by heart, you know what their going through, and you know how making the decision to follow you wont always be easy, but we have that assurance that you are in us, and can heal us, and help us on our Journey. Thank you Jesus for showing me the right way to go, thank you Jesus for never giving up on me. We love you and want to follow you all of our days. Amen

---

John the Baptist Beheaded Mark 6: 14-16

I encourage you to read the whole passage, as I have given you just from 14-16 I believe if you read the rest of the story you can understand more. You can read to the 29th chapter.

King Herod heard about this, for Jesus name has become well known. Some were saying, "John the baptist has been raised from the dead, and that is why miraculous powers are at work in him". Others said, He is Elijah". And still others claimed, He is a prophet, like one of the prophets long ago". But when Herod heard this, he said, "John the man I beheaded, has been raised from the dead!"

So you can only imagine what this king must of thought.

I don't even understand all what is happening in this world we have, but I do understand My Lord and I know he is real, I know he is alive in me. I am going to help you understand this, as much as I can. And this is why I said read the whole story, as it tells more details. And You can gain more understanding.

It is hard, I know we struggle every day, and will until the coming of our great God, our Lord and savour. But we have this assurance that He will come one day and very soon. He said this in the bible and we know this to be true. I am just another woman , person and I am willing to do what God wants me to do, but I can only do this because I have Jesus in my heart and I have the will, (Which Jesus gave me) to do his work here on earth until His comes. I am willing but the body is week, His spirit that is within me, will help me make the right decisions and I can't go wrong there, I just have to put Him who called me first. God must come first over all. Over everything else. If we give up our wills and surrender to His will. Then we will be successful in all our endeavours, praise God for this, as we could not do it if we didn't have the strength that only comes from our Lord Jesus Christ, the God in heaven. Amen

May you be blessed today, may you find your inner peace and may you give your life over to the one who has your best interest at heart.

Thank you Jesus for showing us your great love and Mercies

AND FOR TRUSTING ME TO DO YOUR WORK HERE ON EARTH. Amen

Jesus Feeds the Five Thousand:

Mark 6: 30-44

The apostles gathered around Jesus and reported to him all they had done and taught. Then, because so many people were coming and going that they did not even have time to eat, He said to them, "Come with me by yourselves to a quiet place and get some rest".

So as you read your bible and get closer to him , trust Jesus He knows what he is doing, we are here for him not to be selfish. We need to keep asking Him who knows are hearts and our minds, and our souls. He understands your pain, let it all go to Him, who you can trust, for He has the best for you. and just keep working and doing the will of God and looking unto Him who set us free. We can do all things because God says we can and we must trust him with our all. Everything, lift it up to God to the Lord and Saviour Jesus Christ. Who is and is to come. Forever more. Amen

Lord as I go out to this great unknown please help me to continue to do your will not mine, for I am a child of God and I want to do this, Lord open the doors and close all others, show me the way. Amen

Jesus Walks on the Water

Please make sure you have your bible, note pad and a highlighter and also a pen, I say this because I do this and it helps me in my writing, and for my memory. And then you can write down key notes for yourself. And highlight things in the bible that mean something to you.

Mark 6: 45-56

Immediately Jesus made his disciples get into the boat and go ahead of him to Bethsaida, while He dismissed the crowd. After leaving them, he went up on a mountainside to pray. When evening came, the boat was in the middle of the lake, and he was alone on land. He saw the disciples straining at the oars because the wind was against them. About the fourth hour watch of the night he went out to them, walking on the lake. He was about to pass by them, but when they saw him walking on the lake, they thought he was a ghost. They cried out, because they all saw him and were terrified.

Ya I can see that, I would be like who is that or what is that, I would be scared to.

Immediately he spoke to them and said, "Take courage! It is I. Don't be afraid". Then he climbed into the boat with them, and the wind died down. They were completely amazed, for they had not understood about the loaves; their hearts were hardened.

When the crossed over, they landed at Gennesaret and anchored there. As soon as they got out of the boat, people recognized Jesus. They ran throughout that whole region and carried the sick on mats to wherever they heard he was. And wherever he went-into villages, towns or countryside- they placed the sick in the marketplaces. They begged him to let them touch even the edge of his cloak, and all who touched him were healed.

So you see God can do anything, he understands your misunderstanding, and can help you and I where ever we are, and we don't have to fear because God is always near. He said I will be with you and I will comfort you, and He said we can do all things through Christ and that we must always rely on Him who has our best interest at heart. He would do all things, take a moment now to just let all this sink in.

Lord show us the way, teach us and help us in our own misunderstandings. Help us to continue this path and not go astray, we love you and want to do whats right. We want to follow you, and people tend to steer us wrong, I know they mean well, our loved ones, but they don't know everything. They don't understand us they way you do Lord God, so I pray you would keep us on this strait and narrow path and heal us in our weakness. Thank you Jesus for loving me. Amen

---

Clean and Unclean

Mark 7:1-23

Please always have your bible with you as I may not put the whole verse's in.

The Pharisees and some of the teachers of the law who had come from Jerusalem gathered around Jesus and saw some of the disciples eating food with hands that were "unclean", that is, unwashed. (The Pharisees and all the Jews do not eat unless they give their hands a ceremonial washing, holding to the traditions of the elders. When they came from the marketplace they do not eat unless they wash. And they observe many other traditions, such as washing of cups, pitchers and kettles.) So the Pharisees and teachers of the law asked Jesus, " Why don't you disciples live according to the tradition of the elders instead of eating with their food with unclean hands?" Then He replied, " Isaiah was right when he prophesied about you hypocrites; as it is written:

"These people honor me with their lips, but their hearts are far from me. They worship me in vain; their teachings are but rules taught by men. You have let go of the commandments of God and are holding on to the traditions of man"

Please keep reading your bible. Also if you can try and go out and look for a study bible or something that can help you dive deeper into His word. I found growing up, that it was hard sometimes to read the bible and understand it. So its a good thing to ask for help and look for something that can help you, and always take notes, I try to do that to. Make sure if you are asking people to help you, that you know them personally, as people will try to lead you away.

For today I am going out to enjoy some much needed rest, as I am have been going crazy trying to get my books out there and I really don't know how to do this.

Thank you Lord for helping me to know what to say in my books and for understanding me, now if only you where here in human form you would be able to help me publishing my books and I wouldn't have to struggle to do it alone. Lord please help us all. Amen

The faith of a Syrophoenician Woman

Mark 8: 24-30

Before we begin let me just say a prayer;

Lord please be with everyone who is reading my book and help them understand, Lord please give us peace. Amen

Jesus left that place and went to the vicinity of Tyre. He entered a house and didn't want anyone to know it; yet he could not keep his presence secret. In fact, as soon she heard about him, a woman who's little daughter was possessed by an evil spirit came and fell at his feet. The woman was a Greek, born in Syrian Phoenicia. She begged Jesus to drive the demon out of her daughter. " First let the children eat all they want," he told her, "for it is not right to take the

Children's bread and toss it to their dogs." "Yes Lord," she replied, " but even the dogs under the table eat the children crumbs." Then He told her, "For such a reply, you may go; the demon has left your daughter." She went home and found her daughter lying on the bed, and the demon gone.

Amen to that, Thank you Jesus; You can do All things and we need to let go of all our issues and just trust you with everything, to not worry, You have our backs. We can let go of the pain, and anxiety depression, fear, anything we don't understand. We can just breath and let it all go. For you know what we struggle with and you can heal us. Thank you Jesus for always understanding, for having the power to heal for giving us a hope. I love you Lord God, please be with us all. Help us to always go to you about anything, and know you can help us and we can just trust you with our all. Thank you Lord God. Amen

I have struggled with Anxiety and depression and I have struggled with it most of my life, I also know the Lord is mighty and I do not have to suffer because of this condition, I can just let it all go and know I am going to be okay, I will get through it, the Lord knows what I am going through and I don't have to worry. Thank you Jesus. Amen

Church, I hope my kids go and I hope I can find some peace and get on my way. Lord please go before me and make a way. Lord please give me peace within. Amen

Have you ever have one of those days when you wake up and feel like you didn't sleep and need more sleep? I have and it happen this morning. I thought it was really early, like 3 am so I prayed the Lord would help me sleep a bit more, then I went to the bathroom and when I got back to my bed, I thought what time is it any way, it was 6:30 am. My time to get up. I don't set my alarm on the weekends, so I had to check. And I thought I just want to sleep a bit more, but I new I had to get up soon for church. So I put a sleep story on, while I laid there, I thought why am I trying to go back to sleep when really I should be getting up, So I changed the app to do a Anxiety message for me this am. And then I got up to write. I am glad I did this. My anxiety left me. Amen

This is why its so important to Liston to God, and read His bible, God wants to speak to us through the Holy Spirit we can hear Him. Amen

---

Mark 7: 31-37 The Healing of a Deaf and Mute Man

Then Jesus left the vicinity of the Tyre and went through Sidon, down to the sea of Galilee and into the region of Decapolis. There some people brought to him a man who was deaf and could hardly talk, and they begged him to place his hands the man. After he took him aside, away from the crowd, Jesus put his fingers into the mans ears. Then he spit and touched the mans tongue. He looked up to heaven and with a deep sigh said to him "Ephphatha!" (Which means, Be opened!") At this the mans eyes were opened, his tongue was loosened and he began to speak plainly. Jesus commanded them not to tell anyone. But the more he did so, the more they kept talking about it. The people were overwhelmed with amazement. " He has done everything well," they said. He even makes the deaf hear and the mute speak."

So my question is why would Jesus tell them Not to tell others, I am trying to figure that one out. I will have to ask my pastor, and keep praying about this one. Because in this day and age we must tell people how wonderful Jesus is and how he can heal. So I am struggling with this one. As you read the bible, I think its always important to pray first before you begin reading His word. I believe Jesus will help me understand more and figure things out. So I am not wondering why.

Thank you Jesus for giving me this bible, so I can write and help others on their Journey in this life. My hope is you will continue to help me understand it all. And please Lord I pray you would help me in my weakness so that when I am doing your work, here on earth, that I wouldn't get attacked by the devil. I just want to do your work here Lord and I don't want to fear no more. Amen

Jesus Feeds the Four Thousand:

Mark 8: 1-13

During those days another large crowd gathered. Since they had nothing to eat, Jesus called the disciples to him and said, " I have compassion for these people; they have already been with me three days and have nothing to eat, If I send them home hungry they will collapse on the way, because some of them have come a long distance." His disciples answered, but where in this remote place can anyone get enough bread to feed them?" "How many loafs do you have?" Jesus asked.

Seven they replied.

I will stop there. I have always been fascinated by the number **7**, and what is the significant of the **seven**, I heard people say stuff and I wonder what is it. I will have to get more info to help you understand, and help me know what it really means. Number **seven** has been used in the bible many times, they must be meaning behind it, I will have to ask my pastor to see what he comes up with to. Please read the rest of the paragraph to the end.

As you get to the bottom of the paragraph Jesus asked: " Why does this generation ask for miraculous sign? I tell you the truth, no sign will be given to it."

My own thoughts:

For me that would be a sign Jesus is real and can heal and save, he has shown them that so many times in the bible, I think its a matter of why don't they see the truth its right before their eyes, he is doing amazing and wonderful things, Jesus is showing them, and they must believe, how could they not believe their seeing it with their own eyes. We here in this generation have seen signs and wonders, we see them all the time, and it could be just me, but I know from all the signs that He is real and He will be coming back soon. Be ready, accept him and you shall be free. For we all want a love that will last, His love has lasted all these generations how could we doubt?

My Prayers:

Thank you Jesus for showing us your great mercy and love. We can go from here and help our loved ones knowing you go before us, amen

I am compelled to write, I couldn't sleep and I felt the Lord wanted me to write. So here I am at 1:14 in the am and I am going to tell you whats on my mind. I was laying in bed while listening to some CD of Thunder and nature and I thought about the monkeys in the Morocco and as I listened more to the CD as it brought me to thinking about the Universe and how big it is, and how it would be so cool to go up in space and see the world at a different angle. What a wonder that would be. I want to go and see the world, I have so many dreams; I want to come true, and what I've learned in life, if you want something, you go and get it yourself. I believe that with all my heart, I say a prayer and ask my God to help me to show me the way, to make it come true, if it is His will. And I know he wants me to help as many people as I can to come to know Him as their personal savour, and my dream is to help people on my travels, to talk to as many people as I can. And to learn new hobbies, Its important to keep yourself busy, but not to busy that you forget about your loved ones. We can get caught up in work and play and forget about the ones who love us and may miss us. WE must make the time for them and for our friends. We must put Jesus first, wake in the morning and be thankful that your alive and well, and not to sick, and if your sick and cant work, God knows your situation and will help you. He doesn't want any of his children sick, Sickness doesn't come from God per say, He will heal the sick , comfort the lost and bring home the lonely. He wants whats best for us. He see's whats happening in this world, He allows somethings to happen , I think to teach us something. To show us His great mercy. He is all powerful, all knowing, and he is Supreme. He is my all!

Thank you Jesus for your great love and mercy for me.

Please forgiving me of my sins, Lord you know our hearts, please here our silent cry's and our hopes and dreams, Our hearts cry out to you, we let go and want you to enter in and give us peace. A peace only you can give Lord. Show us there is a better way to do things then what were doing. Help us to let go of the past and leave it behind, help us to forgive our self's, and forgive those who have harmed us. Amen

God is good, all the time.

Lord,; May I be what you want me to be, and may I do it well. Amen

Mark: The Yeast of the Pharisees and Herod

The disciples forgot to bring bread, except for one loaf they had with them in the boat. "Be careful," Jesus warned them. "Watch out for the yeast of the Pharisees and that of Herod."

They discussed this with one another and said, "It is because we have no bread." Aware of their discussion, Jesus asked them: Why are you talking about having no bread? Do you still not see or understand? Are your hearts hardened? Do you have eyes but fail to see, and ears but fail to hear? And don't you remember? When I broke five loaves for the five thousand, how many basket-fuls of pieces did you pick up? " Twelve they replied. " and when I broke the seven loaves for the four thousand, how many basket-ful pieces did you pick up? They answered "seven" He said to them, "Do you still not understand?"

Wow; what a powerful statement. It must of really made them think about their doubting minds. SO you see we shouldn't worry, even the people that were so close to God himself in human form, they still had doubts. We to have them, but we have the Holy Spirit to connect with, and the bible to teach us his word.

Thank you Jesus for your word, it means so much to us. Thank you for giving us peace when we go through the struggles of life, when we are pushed beyond what we think we can handle, you are there, always. We must just go to you and ask for what it is we need, you already know but you want us to talk to you and commune with you. And trust you with our all. Amen

---

Mark 8: 27-30 Peter's Confession of Christ

Jesus and his disciples went on to the villages around Caesarea Philippi. On the way he asked them, " Who do people say I am?" They replied, " Some say John the Baptist; others say Elijah; and still others, one of the prophets."

" But what about you?" He asked. " Who do you say I am?"

Peter answered, "You are the Christ." Jesus warned them not to tell anyone about him.

I often wonder why Jesus would tell them not to go and tell others, weather it be family or friends. I know in this day and age we need to tell others. They are lost and can have a peaceful life if they just except Him and make a better life for themselves. He said you must deny yourself and take up our cross and follow Him. So I am confused with Jesus himself saying; don't tell others, He must know we will. SO what was his purpose? Why would he say that? That's my question for the Pastor. Jesus not only says it once but a few times, and that can be very confusing for a new person of faith. So I must ask the question, not only to my pastor but to my Christian friends.

Jesus is walking and talking with his disciples and with people of all walks of life, so wouldn't He want others to know all the wonders that He himself did? I will keep praying and asking God to help me see and know the answers to my questions.

My Prayer:

Lord show us the way to go, teach us what you want us to learn and help us understand it. Help us to understand your word, because sometimes its really hard to understand. I want to shout out on top of a building, that Jesus is alive in me, He is moving among us and making a difference in our life's, we must share it. We must. Thank you Jesus for saving me, for showing me the way. For loving me and helping me. Amen

---

Mark 8: 31-37 9:1 Jesus predicts His Death

He then began to teach them that the Son of Man must suffer many things and be rejected by the elders, chief priests and teachers of the law, and that he must be killed and after three days rise again. He spoke plainly about this, and Peter took him aside and began to rebuke him. But when Jesus turned and looked at his disciples, he rebuked Peter. "Get behind me Satan!" He said. " You do not have in mind the things of God, but the things of man." Then he called the crowd to him along with his disciples and said: " If anyone would come after me, he must deny himself and take up his cross and follow me. For whoever wants to save his life will lose it, but whoever loses his life for me and the gospel will save it. What good is it for man to gain the whole world, yet forfeit his soul? Or what can a man give in exchange for his soul? If anyone is ashamed of me and my words in this adulteress and sinful generation, the Son of Man will be ashamed of him when he comes in his Fathers glory with his Holy Angels". And He said to them, " I tell you the truth, some who are standing here will not taste death before they see the kingdom of God come with power."

Wow; What a statement. God is all powerful, all knowing, and is the supreme being, He is the only God that can move the mountain in your way, I believe this, you can to, Just trust Him who knows all the hairs on your head, yes everyone of them, even the ones that have fallen. I am amazed every time I read the bible, at how God helps me see the things I need to see and hear the things I need to hear, Thank you Jesus.

I was laying in bed this am, and thought I am OK, I can do this. I don't have to worry, God has a plan for my life. God will move the mountain. Lord show me the way. I need to know this is what you want me to do. I need to know I can get these books published for you and your glory. I want to help as many people as I can to know you and all your wonders, all your understanding. I pray Lord God that you would help me on this journey and give me peace about it. Thank you Lord God. Amen

---

Mark 9:1-13 The Transfiguration

Please read it, this will help you understand what Jesus is trying to tell 3 of his Disciples and he brings them up the mountainside to help them understand. These men must of been really important to Jesus, as he chose them only. We don't know everything what Jesus was thinking, we just know what the good book tells us. I have heard there are other books maybe somewhere in this great big world, that would further our understanding, I will have to do some research on it. And Learn more about it. Till then, we read the bible and ask God to help us understand it. One thing Ive learned in life. Every time I read the bible I learn something new, I ask myself and I pray and ask God to help me understand His word. And He does, He will help you to, he knows our limits and how much it will take for us, he also knows your limits in learning. Just as He has helped me in my learning of His word.

I was watching "Charles Stanley" the other day on T.V. And this is what he was talking about.

"Taking Control of your Thoughts" Colossians 3:1-8 & 6,7

Corinthians 4:3-4

1. You cant control others.
2. Think the right way.
3. Put anger, malice and wrongfulness away.
4. Keep seeking the things above.
5. Set your mind on things above.
6. Trust Jesus
7. Get rid of the greed of things.
8. Put away with bad sins.
9. What you think determines what you do.
10. Learn how to live a Godly life.

The Holy Spirit helps us in our thoughts, and our thoughts have consequences. So try and think rightly. Ask God to help take those stinking thoughts away. I call them stinking because one time when I was doing an anger Management course I had this thought come to my mind, So now when ever I think bad thoughts, I ask God to take away the stinking thoughts and feelings. And I trust He will. The Lord wants whats best for us, He wants us to be happy and live a good life. He also wants us to give our best at all things, and be a good Stewart's of His calling. He has the best in store for you and I. Therefore we must trust Him, he has our best at heart.

We have a self will, don't let others influences us to do wrong, ask God to help us know the difference and keep moving forward, keep looking to the one who has our best interest and to the ones we trust, our family's, what ever that may look like. Walk in the will of God one step at a time, one day at a time, one minute at a time. What ever it takes. Its like doing a 10 step program, one step at a time. Be patient with yourself and with God. He will help you.

Living the Christian life is Rocky.

There are so many traps out there, and people try to trick us into thinking its the right thing to do; what ever it maybe. Ask Jesus to help you see if it is what you should be doing. Ask and then wait, he sometimes take a while to answer, He may have to mould you and help you see what it is you need to do or what you need to change in yourself. Its not always going to be easy, but He knows what He's doing. Stop complaining, read his word, He will show you the way to go. Don t give up on yourself, Rely on the will of God. Your not alone in this and there are people who can help you. Ask God for guidance and He will help you. It takes time to know His will for us.

Ask God to govern your life, ask God for wisdom, in your trials. **Read 1 Peter 3** Learn to trust Him.

Lord show us the way, teach us your will and help us on our way. Amen

---

Mark 9: 33-39 Who Is the Greatest?

They came from Capernaum. When he was in the house, He asked them what were you arguing about on the road?" But the kept quiet because the way they had argued about who was the greatest. Sitting down Jesus called the twelve and said, " If anyone wants to be first, he must be very last, and the servant of all." He took the little child and had him stand among them. Taking him in his arms, he said to them. " Whoever welcomes one of these children in my name welcomes me; and whoever welcomes me does not welcome me but the one who sent me".

Whoever Is Not Against Us Is for Us.

"Teacher", said John, " we saw a man driving out demons in your name and we told him to stop, because he was not one of us." "Do not stop him" Jesus said. No one who does a miracle in my name can in the next moment say anything bad about me, for whoever is not against us is for us. I tell you the truth, anyone who gives you a cup of water in my name because you belong to Christ will certainly not lose his reward.

So you see, we can do things that make a difference, but we must to go to the one who knows us best, and has our interest at hand and wants us to share the good news, with all who will Liston. I am telling you; you can do it, trust Jesus He will be there for you, and help you up out of the muck.

He understands when we have no one to turn to he will always be there. We just need to go to Him. Jesus is the way, the truth, and the hope for our salvation.

My Prayer:

I will do my part Lord, and help as many as I can, show me who needs it and I will do my best, I know you can speak to them through me, for I know not what to say, but you know what they need to here.. Amen

My hope is you can heal and move forward, lets keep reading and learning what it is He wants us to do.

Mark 10: 17-31

As Jesus started on his way, a man ran up to him and fell on his knees before him. "Good teacher," ha asked "What must I do to inherit eternal life?" " Why do you call me good?" Jesus answered. " No one is good-- except God alone. You know the commandments: 'Do not murder, do not commit adultery, do not steal, do not give false testimony, do not defraud, honor your father and mother.' "Teacher", he declared, " all these I have kept since I was a boy." Jesus looked at him and loved him. "One thing you lack," he said. "Go, sell everything and give to the poor, and you will have treasures in heaven. Then come, follow me."

At this the mans face fell. He went away sad, because he had great wealth. Jesus looked around and said to his disciples, "How hard is it for the rich to enter the Kingdom of God?"

The disciples were amazed at his words. But Jesus said again, "Children how hard is it to enter the kingdom of God! It is easier for a camel to go through the eye of a needle then for a rich man to enter the kingdom of God."

The disciples were amazed at His teaching, and were talking to each other about all that was said. And they asked themselves, who then can be saved?

Jesus looked at them and said: " With man this is impossible, but not with God; all things are possible with God."

Please keep reading; the story just keeps getting better.

My bible has Jesus's words in red so I know who is talking, it helps. When I first started reading the bible I had a hard time understanding it, So if I may suggest, when you get a bible please look for one that is a study bible, it will help you a lot. And maybe one that has red lettering when Jesus is speaking. I got a woman's bible, and I have found that it has helped, I think it is good to have something that can guide you and help you on your faith Journey. I am still looking for one that can keep me on the right track, keep me learning. And teach me more about Jesus.

There are many churches that may provide a good bible, or even give you one. And there are many stores that carry them to. Do some research on finding the right one for you. Its important to keep your faith strong, and keep moving towards Jesus.

Lord Show us your ways, that we may follow you, until the end of day. Amen

---

Mark 10:35-45 The Request of James and John

Then James and John, the sons of Zebedee, came to him. "Teacher," they said, "we want you to do for us whatever we ask,." "What do you want me to do for you? He asked. They replied, "Let one of us sit at your right and the other at your left in glory." "You don't know what your asking," Jesus said.

"Can you drink the cup I drink or be baptized with the baptism I am baptized with, but to sit at my right or my left is not for me to grant. These places belong to those for whom they have been prepared."

Please keep reading the rest of the story.

I am kinda shocked at the fact they asked Jesus to sit at his right and left in heaven, I mean I don't think we are worthy enough to sit by his side in heaven, but I believe he will let us sit down and he would sit right beside us. I think James and John were very bold to ask that question. Makes me wonder. As I am sure you would wonder to, and I can see why their friends became indignant with them, like how dare they. But I guess they felt worthy enough and strong enough to ask that question. And maybe it was something on their minds for awhile. All we know is, they felt worthy enough to ask the question. I know God heals and forgives; so I am just happy to know he has forgiven me and that I am going to make it to heaven, that is enough for me. Now I must do his work and help as many as I can to find the Lord, for he loves us all. And wants all to come to know Him. So please tell your friends and family about the Love of God and Jesus His one and only son; that He came to earth to save us from ourselves, He came to heal the sick and give hope to the hopeless. Jesus Is Love, and wants whats best for us, He came here from far away and brought Love. And gives if freely, Jesus is the hope for us all; from this fallen world we live in. God made these planets and everything in the universe, So he is the almighty, the ever lasting God. And will come to our rescue. It may take time, for we has humans want it now, and He knows when the right time is. God is all powerful all knowing, all supreme. He knows all and can fix your problems, just trust Him and your life will get better. Amen

My Prayer:

Lord show us your ways, so we may follow you and be good and faithful Stuarts. Help us in our troubles and give us peace, Amen

---

Mark 11: 20-25 The withered Fig Tree

In the morning, as they went along, they saw the fig tree withered from the roots. "Rabbi, look! The fig tree you cursed has withered!" "Have faith in God," Jesus answered. " I tell you the truth, if anyone says to this mountain, 'Go, throw yourself into the sea,' and does not doubt in his heart but believes what he says will happen, it will be done for him. Therefore I tell you, believe that you have received it, and it will be yours. And when you stand praying, if you hold anything against anyone, forgive him, so that your Father in heaven may forgive you your sins."

What does this mean to you?, how do you feel about this question? Will you look to God and ask forgiveness and seek His face, I say yes! We can look to Jesus for anything, He may not give it to us right away or at all, but He knows whats best for us, He knows the future. And I trust him.

I will be studying 1 peter as I am now in a bible study course, and I want to learn more, where shall I go from here, I am not certain, but I know God has a plan for me and will reveal it to me soon I hope. I will be starting a new course soon, maybe one for teaching I don't know. I do want to help as many people as I can, so maybe teaching or something, along those lines.

May God richly bless you today, and may you find peace within.

Lord show us the way, teach us I pray. Amen

Mark 12:13-17 Paying Taxes to Caesar

You can read 12:1 just to see what Jesus was talking about before you read the 13th chapter.

Later they sent some of the Pharisees and Herodians to Jesus to catch him in his words. They came to him and said, "Teacher, we know you are a man of integrity. You aren't swayed by man, because you pay no attention to who they are; but you teach the way of God in accordance with the truth. Is it right to pay taxes to Caesar or not? Should we pay or shouldn't we?" But Jesus knew their hypocrisy, "Why are you trying to trap me?" He asked. "Bring me denarius and let me look at it." They brought the coin, and asked them. "Whose portrait is this?" And whose inscription?" "Caesar's," they replied. Then Jesus said to them, "Give to Caesar what is Caesar's and to God what is God's." And they were amazed at him.

Yes Jesus is amazing, and His wonder's are many, we cannot fathom how wide and how far they are for us. Jesus is the great; and all knowing. He can and will help us when we struggle and in our every day life, just call on his name and he will be there for you. We must always put Him for first, for if we do, He will be there for us always. Yes always, He may not answer the way we want, or when; but He knows whats best for us. Sometimes we ask for things he knows we do not need. He knows whats best, and wants the best for us. Sometimes his answer takes a while, maybe we are not ready yet, maybe he has to work things out for you, before He answers you. Maybe He has to change something within us so we can be good at it. What ever the reason, we must wait upon the Lord, we must or we will get ahead of our-self's and it may not be right for us. So please ask, then wait. He will answer. In due time. His timing is always right. This is where we learn patients, and integrity. Jesus knows us, remember He want's what's best for us, and will go to great lengths to help us, and has been there since the beginning. He knows all and has the power to change us and help us in our situations.

Dear Lord;

Please go before us today, help us make the right decisions and do the right things, show us the way Oh Lord and help us to be more patient with our self's, with you and others. Amen

A poem:

I couldn't tell you how it felt when they ripped the beard from His face.
I couldn't tell you how it felt when they nailed Him in my place.
I couldn't tell you how it felt when they ripped the clothes from His back.
Could you imagine how it feels to sweat blood like that?

Take Him down from the tree; wipe His wounds that should be on me.
I am a criminal yet you take my place.
Jesus, how I love you. Jesus, how I love you.

All alone on a tree, not even one disciple found at all.
As my master lies between to thieves, Oh God forgive us all.

Take Him down from the tree; wipe His wounds that should be on me.
I am a criminal yet you take my place.
Jesus, how I love you. Jesus, how I love you.

And the next time my God appears, He won't be alone.
He will come in power, and you will see Him and know Him,
That Jesus is the Lord of all. I know.

When you walked with your cross to Calvary,
A painful reminder of what you did for me.
I began crying, pictured you dying,
But those words you said, "Father forgive them."
I'm forgiven.

Take Him down from the tree; wipe His wounds that should be on me.
I am a criminal yet you take my place.
Jesus, how I love you. Jesus, how I love you.
Auther unknown.

---

1 Peter 3:3, 12-17 Praise to God for a Living Hope

Please read all of 1Peter 3 to 17. 1 peter 2 1-2

Praise be to the God and Father of our Lord Jesus Christ! In his great mercy He has given us new birth into a living hope through the resurrection of Jesus Christ from the dead, and into an inheritance that can never parish, spoil or fade-kept in heaven for you, who through faith are shielded by God's power until the coming of the salvation that is ready to be revealed in the last time. In this you greatly rejoice, though now for a little while you may have had to suffer grief in all kinds of trials. These have come, so that your faith-of greater worth then gold, which parishes even though refined by fire-may be proved genuine and may result in praise, glory and honor when Jesus Christ is revealed. Though you have not seen him; you love him; and even though you do not see him now, you believe in him and are filled with inexpressible and glorious joy, for you are receiving the goal of your faith, the salvation of your souls.

Being Holy:

He talks about being Holy, what does that mean to you? Do you feel holy, can you write it down what it means to you to be holy? See where it takes you and then keep reading the bible. To 17

1 Peter 2

Therefore, rid yourself of all malice and all deceit, hypocrisy, envy, and slander of every kind. Like newborn babies, crave spiritual milk, so that by it you may grow up in your salvation, now that you have tasted that the Lord is good.

Keep praying, keep hoping and never give up the fight for your right to freedom. Do what you need to do; keep fighting till you find that peace and that hope you so desire. Never give up the hope that you have found in Jesus! He is the one and only one who can lift you up and keep you going. He will give you power and get you where He wants you to be.

Lord show us where you want us and reveal to us your hope and yourself to us, that we may feel your love and kindness. We hope for the future, we hope for peace and look forward to your coming. Amen

---

1 Peter 2:13-22 Submission to Rulers and Masters

Submit yourselves for the Lords sake to every authority insitited among men: weather to the king, as supreme authority, or to governors, who are sent by him to punish those who do wrong and to commend those who do right. For it is Gods will that by doing good you should silence the ignorant talk of foolish men. Live as free men, but do not use your freedom as a cover up for evil; live as servants of God. Show proper respect to everyone: Love the brotherhood of believers, fear God, honor the King.

Keep reading the rest of the verses. And stop and just ask God to help u understand it all. As It can be misunderstood, and I believe God wants this to be understood as He wants us all to understand his words. His promises; God is a just God, and we should be so thankful for all that he has done for us.

In my bible; I have woman Authors who put there little tid bits in, here is one for you today.

Living a Holy Life

Have you had difficultly with this scripture verse: "Be Holy, because I am Holy" (Leviticus 11:44; 1 Peter 1:16)? Since most people think being holy is synonymous with being sinless, who possible be holy? It's unattainable...unimaginable! A friend once said to me, "I know holy means set apart, but I dont want to be set apart. That sounds like being in quarantine for having a constant case of measles!" Some people do think of a holy person as one who lives as a monkish existence, praying ever, does not bring isolation but integration. With Christ in you, his character becomes part of you so that his nature may be expressed through you. In other words, Christlikeness will come out of you naturally. When I was little, my uncle Jimmy walked me through his watermelon patch in Idabel, Oklahoma. Holding a tiny black seed he said, "These big melons grew from seeds just like this one". That seemed impossible to me! Yet eighty miles from Idabel is Hope, Arkansas, the town where something more "impossible" became reality, Young Jason Bright gave his watermelon seed proper care and the right environment to grow, The result? A world-record 260 pounds watermelon! Watermelon seeds simply do what comes naturally to them-they grow. Their seeds are set apart by God for that purpose. When you are set apart by God, holiness becomes natural. The father is the gardener; Christ is the seed. With Christ in you, you will grow to be like him. It is explained in 1 John 3:9

No one who is born of God will continue to sin, because God's seed remains in him.

It is natural for the Lord not to sin. Therefore, with God's seed in you, it becomes increasingly natural for you not to sin. What seems impossible becomes possible. You will not become instantly sinless, but you will sin less and less. God calls you holy. With his presence inside you, he will produce the impossible through you. Why settle for anything less?

So Go out there and make a difference today, give someone a big hug, give someone a hand shake, tell someone they are special to you. And start to make a difference today, why wait.

My Prayer;

Lord show us the way and teach us I pray. Help us to give and not be so ignorant to others. Amen

---

1 Peter 4:1-11 Living for God

Therefore, since Christ suffered in his body, arm yourselves also with the same attitude, because he who has suffered in his body is done with sin. As a result, he does not live the rest of his earthly life for evil human desires, but rather for the love of God. For you have spent enough time in the past doing what pagans choose to do-living in debauchery, lust, drunkenness, orgies, carousing in detestable idolatry. They think it strange that you do not plunge with them into the same flood of dissipation, and they heap abuse on you. But they will have to give account to who is ready to judge the living and the dead. For this is the reason the gospel was preached even to those who are now dead, so that they might be judged according to God in regard to the spirit. The end of all things is near, therefore be clear minded and self-controlled so that you can pray. Above all, love each other deeply, because love covers over a multitude of sins. Offer hospitality to one another without grumbling. Each one should use what ever gift he has received to serve others, faithfully administering Gods grace in various forms. If anyone speaks he should do it as one speaking the very words of God. If anyone serves, he should do it with the strength God provides, so that in all things God may be praised through Jesus Christ. To him be the glory and the power for ever and ever Amen.

Ask yourself these questions:

How am I feeling?
What am I angry about?
Anxious about?
Glad about?
Happy about?

Write the answers down and reflect on them.
Then ask, " How is God speaking to me through these feelings"?

My Prayer;

Lord; thank you for your word, may I be ever so bold to speak it out loud and give direction to the lost amen.

---

2 Peter 5:12-15 prophecy of Scripture

So I will always remind you of these things, even though you know them and are firmly established in the truth you now have. I think it is right to refresh your memory as long as I live in this tent of his body, because I know that I will soon put it aside, as our Lord

Jesus Christ has made clear to me. And I will make every effort to see that after my departure you will always be able to remember these things.

Self-sacrifice

"Be completely humble and gentle; be patient, bearing with one another in Love" (Ephesians 4:2)

Love demonstrates itself in action. Self-sacrifice is against our human nature, yet it should be part of our "New nature"

If each of us had an attitude of self sacrifice, what a change would come about in the atmosphere of our homes.

Self-sacrifice is total unselfishness. Loving unselfishly does not mean making the least of ourselves but making the most of someone else. We view the other person through the eyes of Jesus.

This can transform our thoughts and our homes. Is it worth it, Yes it is.

Lord show us the way and teach us right from wrong. Help us to give ourselves up to you daily, and to help others always. Amen

---

Colossians 3: 2, 5-9 and 12-14 3:23 Rules for Holy Living.

Set your minds on things above, not on earthly things.

Put to death, therefore, whatever belongs to your earthly nature: Sexual immorality, impurity, lust, evil desires and greed, which is idolatry. Because of these, the wrath of God is coming. You use to walk in these ways, in the life you once lived, now you must rid your self of all such things as these: anger, rage, malice, slander and filthy language from your lips. Do not lie to each other.

Verse 12 to15

Clothes yourself with Compassion, kindness, humility, gentleness and patience.

Keep reading it.

And the **verse 23** Whatever you do, work at it with all your heart, as working for the Lord, not for men,

You can continue to read the rest. It is very interesting and informative. We must keep reading, as when we are in His word, thats when we can learn and grow. And we can learn to fight the battles of every day life!

My prayer:

Lord show me the way today, and help me to be strong and to make the right decisions today. Amen

---

2 Peter: 7,8,9,10,11 . The day of The Lord

By the same word the present heavens and earth are reserved for fire, being kept for the day of judgment and destruction of ungodly men. But do not forget this one thing, dear friends: With the Lord a day is like a thousand years, and a thousand years like a day. The Lord is not slow in keeping his promise, as some understand slowness. He is patient with you, not wanting anyone to parish, but everyone to come to repentance. But the day will come like a thief. The heavens will disappear with a roar; the elements will be destroyed by fire and the earth and everything in it will be laid bare. Since everything will be destroyed in this way, what kind of people ought you to be? You ought to live holy and godly lives.

Yes we should live holy and godly lives, we should watch what we say to people, they could be an angel sent from God to teach us something, and we wouldn't want to talk down to an angel of God, we must watch our steps, and be diligent in our living. We must treat each other with kindness and love, we must because that's how God originally made us to be, like Him and full of love and acceptance. Full of kindness, and forgiveness, we must forgive to live a rightly life. God forgave us so we must learn to forgive those who harmed us. We can if we first ask God to forgive us, and help us in this. For some of you this is a daunting task, and it may seem very hard, but once you let God in and He begins His transformation in you you will want to forgive, and keep forgiving. You will be a changed person, people will see it, some will run; some will want what you have. Give freely as God gave freely to you. And Life will get better. God will open your eyes again to see the light. He will give you peace. Amen to that.

I am finding it hard some days to keep going, as a new writer and with know knowledge to know how to start or where to go and with whom can I trust, it is a very daunting task and I am not always up for it, I struggle to write some days, to know what to say, or how to say it; I am thinking this book has a lot of references' to the bible but I am I not telling my story right?, have I failed you by not telling you more about me?, or how my life is? I hope I have given you hope and I hope my writing isn't boring, that would be a great tragedy and a loss to me, so I need to talk , more about me, and my journey. I have to look back on what I have learned over the years from people places and things, and I see that I am always learning new things, I remember having a thought when I was a young one, that "I have done my schooling and done learning", but life is learning, we are always learning new things, It took me like

30 years to realize this, when I did I started to learn more because I was open to learning more. I didn't realize I was closing myself of to learning new things by saying I am done learning, because I was ignorant to it. And I didn't realize it, I was still young and ignorant to it all. We live we learn, I remember someone once saying this, we live we learn. So as long as we are living we are learning, always. Amen to that. God gave a us a brain so we must keep learning new things to keep on top of things. Life is a journey and I want mine to be a good one from now on.

Oh Lord help me to look to you for all my answers, may you send people in my life whom I can learn from and whom I can teach. Amen

My Prayer:

Lord help us to forgive those that have hurt us deeply, help us to forgive completely from the bottom of our souls. And help us help our enemies. For they to need forgiveness to; For this is the right thing to do. Thank you God for forgiving me. Amen

---

1 John:5-10 Walking in the light

This is the message we have heard from him and declare to you. God is light; in him there is no darkness at all. If we claim to have fellowship with him yet walk in darkness we lie and do not live by the truth. But if we walk in the light, we have fellowship with one another, and the blood of Jesus, his son, purifies us from all sin. If we claim to be without sin we deceive ourselves and the truth is not in us. If we confess our sins, he is faithful and just and forgives us of our sins and purify us from all unrighteousness. If we claim we have not sinned, we make him out to be a liar and his word has no place in our lives.

This is a pretty hard for some to understand and do, but we must confess and bring it to Him who knows all and wants us to confess so he can forgive us. So we can be set free, and be free indeed! Yes we all want to have that freedom, and be clear of who we are, so we must keep going to the Father and asking for forgiveness, it is what we should be doing every day. God breathed his word into these men and woman so we could have the bible, and be free to. So we must keep living for Him who has our best interest at hand.

My prayer:

Lord you know my struggles and my pain please heal me and help me cope with the every day things, show me how to deal with people in general, Lord show me who I need today, show me who I can help today and please forgive me of my sins. Amen

Lets continue to do His work here till it is our time to leave this earth.

REJOICE

In heavenly love abiding, No change my heart shall fear;
And safe is such confiding, For nothing changes here.
The storm may roar without me, My heart may low be laid,
But God is round about me, And I can be dismayed?
Wherever He may guide me, No fear shall turn me back;
My shepherd is beside me, and nothing shall I lack.
His wisdom ever waketh, His sight is never dim;
He knows the way he taketh, An I will walk with Him.
Green pastures are before me, Which yet I have not seen;

Bright skys will soon be o'er me, where darkest clouds have been. My hope I cannot measure, My path to life is free;

My savior is my treasure, And He will walk with me.

Anne L. Waring

---

1 John 2:18-27 Warning Against Antichrists

Dear Children this is the last hour; and as you have heard that the antichrist is coming, even now many antichrist have come. This is how we know it is the last hour. They went out from us, but they did not really belong to us. For is they had belong to us, for if they had belonged to us, they would have remained with us; but their going showed that none of them belong to us. But you have an anointing from the Holy One, and all of you know the truth, but because you do know it and because no lie comes form the truth. Who is the liar? It is the man who denies that Jesus is the Christ. Such a man is the antichrist-he denies the Father and the Son. No who denies the Son has the Father; whoever acknowledges the Son has the Father also. See that what you have heard from the beginning remains in you. If it does, you also will remain in the Son and in the father. And this is what He promised us-even eternal life. I am writing these things to you about those who are trying to lead you astray. As for you, the anointing you received from him remains in you, and you do not need anyone to teach you. But as his anointing teaches you about all things and as that anointing is real, not counter-feit just as it has taught you, remain in Him.

We are children of God and no one can snatch us away, no one! We are His and His forever. Amen

Dear children, do not let anyone lead you astray The reason the Son of God appeared was to destroy the devils work.

So lets be diligent in our prayer life and keeping the commandments set for us. We can succeed and we can do it with the power He gives us, we can be conquerors in Christ and He will give us what we need at the time we need it. And He will go before us and make a way, He will give us hope and courage and what ever it is we may need at the time. That power is absolutely yours, by faith. Take it and head out. The victories are just beginning. There is power is Jesus Name.

My Prayer:

Dear Lord please be with us as we face the daily challenges of life and give us hope and courage to keep going, turn the evil one away and give us Joy. Lord show us the way to go. Amen

---

Daniel 10:1-21 Daniel's Vision of a Man

I will start with the 4th verse, Please read from the first until the 21, Its a lot to write out so I will put in here what I have highlighted in my bible.

On the twenty-fourth day of the first month, as I was standing on the bank of the great river, the Tigris, I looked up and there before me was a man dressed in linen, with a belt as finest gold around his waist. His body like chrysolite, his face like lightning, his eyes like flaming torches, his arms and legs like the gleam of burnished bronze, and his voice like the sound of multitude. I, Daniel, was the only one who saw the vision; the men with me did not see it, but such terror overwhelmed that they fled and hid themselves. So I was left alone gazing at this great vision, I had know strength left, my face turned deathly pale and I was helpless. Then

I heard him speaking, and as I listen to him, I fell into a deep sleep, my face to the ground.

Keep reading His word, as you do He will give you wisdom. And will take away all your fears, ask Him and he will help you understand.

Some of the old testaments are hard to understand, I find once you get closer to God and keep reading his word, you will gain strength and wisdom, God will help you though it. I still have a hard time with the old testaments and I tend to read more of the new then the old. I ask for guidance and hope God will help me get to the point of understanding more of the old books. And my hope is that I continue to be strong in my faith and be open to learning more and gaining more wisdom. I hope this book and my first book has helped you on your journey. May you find peace and happiness in your daily walk with him. Amen

My Prayers:

Lord show us your will and keep us safe today, may we gain more understanding of your word and what you want us to do in our walk with you, may we sense your loving arms around us always. Amen

---

Hosea 11:1-11 God's Love for Israel

I am only going to write a few lines, then I want you to read the rest in your bible.

"When Israel was a child, I loved him, and out of Egypt I called my son. But the more I called Israel, the further they went from me. They sacrificed to baals and they burned incense to images.

And He will settle them in their homes. Declares the Lord!

Compassion Is Active!

Christian's are sometimes accused of being so heavenly minded that they are no earthly good. We get caught up in choir rehearsals, studies of the end times or other church activities, and ignore needs around us. When problems are brought to out attention, we content ourselves with feeling sorry about them while doing nothing. But sympathic thoughts or kindly musings are not true compassion. With the divine power He possessed, Jesus could of met the multitudes needs merely by forming a thought or speaking a command. He could of even done that from heaven without coming to earth. But his compassion caused him not only to come and live and die among us, but also to touch lepers

(Mark 1:40-41) and blind men (Matthew 20:34), and to take little children in his arms (Mark 10:13-16). True compassion is personal, active involvement that expresses God's merciful heart in words and deeds. God's chosen people to "Clothe" themselves with compassion (Colossians 3:12). We are to meet others needs, not to continually satisfy our selfish desires. As God showers us with comfort through his Word and through other believers, we in turn are to redirect the stream of his mercy to others. We are not to hoard God's love, but to overflow with the good news of his compassion to all.

So you see we must keep forgiving and giving, and loving. We must and when we do we feel the love back; we get when we give, when I give I get joy; seeing how happy I made someone, that's pure Joy!

Joel 2:12-14, 21-23 Rend Your Heart

"Even now," declares the Lord "return to me with all your heart, with fasting and weeping and mourning."

Rend your heart and not your garments. Return to the Lord your God for He is graces and compassionate, slow to anger and abundant in love, and He relents from sending calamity. Who knows? he may turn and have pity and leave behind a blessing- grain offerings and drink offerings for the Lord your God.

Verse 21-23

Surely he has done great things. Be not afraid, O land; be glad and rejoice. Surely the Lord has done great things. Be not afraid, O wild animals for the open pastures are becoming green. The trees are bearing their fruit; the fig trees and vine yield their riches. Be glad, O people of Zion, rejoice in the Lord your God, for He has given you the autumn rains in righteousness. He sends you abundant showers, both autumn and spring rains as before.

So remember the rain stops and the flowers come, we will be like that of the flower, we will bloom again and shower our love to those around us, we will be strong in His name again. Life will keep moving, and we will be strong. Stronger then before, then ever before! The Lord is mighty and He has saved us from our sins. He has changed us forever and we will shine and move on.

I can is what we should say, or I will try and do it, what ever it may be; we can bring joy again to those around us. Jesus loves me this I know. For the bible tells me so.

My Prayers:

Lord help us to be strong in your name, help us to keep looking forward and not back, help us this day Amen

Psalms1:1-3 12:7, 8

Blessed is the man who does not walk in the counsel of the wicked or stand in the way of sinners or sit in the seat of mockers. But his delight is in the law of the Lord, and on his law he meditates day and night. He is like a tree planted by streams of water, which yields its fruit in season and whose leaf does not wither. Whatever he does prospers.

O Lord, you will keep us safe and protect us from such people forever. The wicked freely strunt about when what is vile is honored among men.

I keep looking back at the bible and I say to myself I should try and read the old testaments more, but I have a hard time with it. So much killing and wars, and Jesus wasn't yet born so there was a lot of evil present. I find it hard to understand. I do love the Psalms and many other books in the old testaments, I just find it hard to understand, and hard to except. I like Deuteronomy it has some very interesting things. The Lords commandments are there and it helps me understand some of it.

Lets talk about the 10 commandments; It maybe hard to do some for some people, like Honor your Father and mother, how does one do that if they are the ones beating you and hurting you? Or how do you not ever never steal, I am sure everyone has stolen something in there life time. These commandments are hard, but necessary and it hold us accountable. We must do what the Lord wants of us, if we want to do what's right and have a hard time; ask the Lord to help you to kick the bad habit, like smoking or drinking, or any other deeds that we know are bad. We can stop with His help and the help of others around us. Those ones who claim to be there for us take them up on it, ask for help. And tell them how you need them. If you don't have family for what ever reason, look to the elderly they have a lot of knowledge. Join a support group, they often have a lot of help and if they cant help they can direct you to help. But mostly look to the bible, it has everything you need for life; the right life. A good life. A happy life!

My prayers:

Dear Lord show us the way and teach us I pray, help us to keep going especially when it's really hard to, show us there is a way out of the situations we got ourselves into, Lord help us I pray. Amen

---

Matthew 18:1-9 The Greatest in the Kingdom of Heaven

Please read it.

The Parable of the Lost Sheep Verse 10-14

See that you do not look down on one of these little ones. For I tell you that their angels in heaven always see the face of my Father in heaven. What do you think? If a man owns a hundred sheep, and one of them wonders away, will he not leave the ninety nine on the hills and go look for the one that wondered off? And if he finds it, I tell you the truth, he is happier about that one sheep than about the ninety-one that did not wonder off. In the same way your Father in heaven is not willing that any of these little ones should be lost.

So you see He does care for us all, He wants what's best for us, He wants us to follow Him till the end, and be strong in His name, and forgive those that have harmed us and hurt us; lets remember the Lord in all that we do, lets put Him first always, and be thankful. For He is always watching over us and only lets things happen, because He knows we can handle it. He only gives us as much as we can handle, nothing more.

My Prayers:

Lord show us your ways help us to follow you till the end, help us to keep forgiving others that have harmed us, help us show the mercy you showed us, to others, to forgive them, and love them. Amen

---

Matthew 18: 15-20 A Brother Who Sins Against You

If your brother sins against you, go and show him his fault, just between the two of you. If he listens to you, you have won your brother over. But if he will not listen, take one or two others along, so that every matter may be established by the testimony of two or three witnesses. If he refuses to listen to them, tell it to the church; if he refuses to even listen to the church, treat him as you would a pagan or a tax collector. I tell you the truth, what ever you bind on earth will be bond in heaven, and whatever you loose on will be loosed in heaven. "Again, I tell you that if two of you on earth agree about anything you ask for, it will be done for you by my Father in heaven. For where two or three come together in my name, there am I with them." Thank you Jesus.

Walking in His presence is important to me, and I feel better when I am with the Lord, I am glad He excepted me into his home in heaven. I am great-full for my mom bringing me to her friends home so I can be saved. My life may have not gotten better after that,(Only because I wasn't faithful in following him) but I realized as I got older how important it was to be close to Him, and wait for the things I wanted or needed. I am still learning to be patient, its hard sometimes when its something you have been waiting for or wanting for a long time. But I am learning, life is about learning. And I believe God has big plans for you and I, I believe God can move that mountain, we just need the faith, and courage to keep going. To never give up the fight, to keep leaning on Him. And If I get lost I know where to turn.

My Prayers:

Dear Lord, please go before us and make a way, help us in our daily walk with you, help us to rely on you and look to you when we need something. For you know what we need before we ask; you understands our needs, and you want to help us. Lord help us to be a good example to all those around us. Show us the way and teach us, I pray. Amen

---

Matthew 24:1-14 Signs of the End of the Age

Jesus left the temple and was walking when his disciples came up to him and called his attention to its buildings.

"Do you see these things?" he asked. "I tell you the truth, not one stone here will be left on another; every one will be thrown down." As Jesus was sitting on the mount of Olives, the disciples came to him privately. "Tell us," they said, "when will this happen, and what will be the sign of your coming and of the end of age?" Jesus answered; " Watch out that no one deceives you. For many will come in my name, claiming, I am the Christ and will deceive many. You will hear wars and rumors of wars, but see to it you are not alarmed. Such things must happen, but the end is still to come, nation will rise against nation, and kingdom against kingdom. There will be famines and earthquakes in various places. All these are the beginning of the birth pains. Then you will be handed over to be persecuted and put to death, and you will be hated by all nations because of me. At that time many will turn from the faith and will betray and hate each other, and many false prophets will appear and deceive many people. Because of the increase of wickedness, the love of most will grow cold, but he who stands firm to the end will be saved. And this gospel of the Kingdom will be preached in the whole world as a testimony to all nations, and then the end will come. Wow

This is a profound statement, and one to ponder, we must be patient and open to hearing what God has to say to us, we must put all evil aside and follow Jesus, we must keep our faith, if anyone is week ask for strength, if anyone is afraid we must ask for faith to believe God will defend us and give us hope. He will be there for you when you fall. Just don't give up hope, even if you feel like there is know hope, just ask God to give you hope and to help you.

My Prayers:

Lord help me in my decisions and give me guidance, as I need you day and night. I need you all the time. Lord help us forgive ourselves for the sins we have done, help us to have the courage to ask for forgiveness and to give it. Lord I want to be kind and good, show me the way. Amen

---

Mark 4:3-9 The parable of the Sower

Listen! A Farmer went out to sow his seed. As he was scattering the seed, some fell among the path, and the birds came and ate it all up. Some fell on rocky places, where it did not have much soil.

It sprang up quickly, because the soil was shallow. But when the sun came up, the plants were scorched, and they withered because they had no root. Other seed fell among thorns, which grew up and chocked the plants, so they did not bear grain. Still other seed fell on good soil. It came up, grew and produced a crop, multiplying thirty, sixty, or even a hundred times. Then Jesus said, "He who has ears to hear, let him hear."

The meaning; We need to go plant the seed, tell people about Jesus and his love, they may need Him more then we know, we all need him, just some of us are to stubborn to turn from our sins and repent. Jesus is calling, He wants all to come to know him, and why wouldn't you want that, God is love and we all want love. Right? So go out there, seek the lost and tell them the good news! Jesus loves them, they are loved and valued. And they can be found, they can be somebody, they are not alone. We get so caught up in our daily lives that we forget to help the ones who are seeking, who are wanting to feel loved. Who need his love, I feel I can make a difference in many peoples lives, if I just get out of my own way. Amen!

My prayers:

Dear Lord, show me who it is that needs you today, and please give me the right words to say, Amen

---

Matthew 12:33 Jesus is talking

Make a tree good and its fruit will be good, or make a tree bad and its fruit will be bad, for a tree is recognized by its fruit. You brood of vipers, how can you who are evil say anything good? For out of the overflow of the heart of the mouth speaks. The good man brings good things out of the good stored up in him, and the evil man brings evil things out of the evil stored up in him. But I tell you that men will have to give account on the day of Judgment for every carless word they have spoken. For by your words you will be acquitted, and by your words you will be condemned."

This can be scary for someone who has said a lot of bad things, and for someone who has a truckers mouth, at least that's what I've heard them say, that truckers say a lot of bad words. I use to when I was a teen, I was lost and was not fallowing Jesus, I was rebelling and not following the way of the Lord, I was following the ways of the world. Doing things I would rather not repeat. I hurt people with my tongue I am sure. And words hurt. This is why its so important to keep going to church and reading His word, if we want change, we must read his word day and night; and go to church, a church that worships Jesus Christ. And do the right things, we cant get to heaven from the goods we do, we must except Jesus and then ask for Guidance along the way! Thank you Jesus

My prayers:

Lord help us to keep coming to you all the time, help us to know you understand and are there to help us and guide us, help us to know we can come to you about anything, after all you know what we have done and what we have said. And you still love us unconditionally, that is something, because a lot of people don't even know what its like to feel the love, I cant even imagine going through life without love, how hard that would be. Jesus is love, you give it freely; we reach out every day and ask for it Lord. I believe in you Jesus to help us all the time, help us give up our stubbornness and give up our own wills and follow You lord God. I know I need you, without you I am nothing. Jesus you have made me whole again. Thank you Jesus, Amen

Matthew 13:31

The Parables of the Mustard Seed and the Yeast

Before you read this one, please go back to **Matthew 24** and read the parable of the weeds.

He told them another parable: " The kingdom of heaven is like a mustard seed, which a man took and planted in his field. Through it is the smallest of all your seeds, yet when it grows, it is the largest of the garden plants and becomes a tree, so that the birds of the air come and perch on its branches." He told them still another parable: "The kingdom is like yeast that a woman took and mixed into a large amount of flour until it worked all through the dough." Jesus spoke all these things to the crowd in parables; he did not say anything to them without using a parable. So was fulfilled what was spoken through prophet:

"I will open my mouth in parables, I will utter things hidden since the creation of the world." Now I want you to read the Parable of the weeds explained. **Matthew 36**

Just so you get an understanding of the parables and its meanings. I want you to understand what Jesus is saying, and how we must ask God for understanding of His word, we must ask God first and then go forth. And I pray you will understand and grow in your faith journey.

My Prayers:

Dear Lord; please help us in our walk with you, show us the way and help us I pray, Lord you know our hearts, you know us completely, help us to know you and learn of your ways; teach us I pray Amen

Matthew 13:47-52 The Parable of the Net

"Once again, the kingdom of heaven is like a net that was let down into the lake and caught all kinds of fish. When it was full, the fisherman pulled it up on the shore. Then they sat down and collected the good fish in baskets, but threw the bad away. This is how it will be at the end of age. The angels will come and separate the wicked from the righteous and throw them into the fiery furnace, where there will be weeping and gashing of teeth. " Have you understood all these things?" Jesus asked. "Yes," they replied. He said to them, "Therefore every teacher of the law who has been instructed about the kingdom of heaven is like the owner of a house who brings out of his storeroom new treasures as well as old".

So we must keep our faith and keep doing good, and looking to God for our guidance.

Did you know Jesus had siblings? He did, and in the bible it tells of his brothers but not of his sisters, at least I haven't read of it yet. His brothers were, James, Joseph, Simon, and Judas. That's what it says in Matthew. I often wondered how they felt, being a brother to someone so special, someone who has such power! I wonder how they felt. We are all sister and brother in Christ, but they were flesh and bones. And for me that is amazing; and exciting knowing he had siblings, and he new what it was like to have a real brother and sister. So He understands how we feel. Even though He was God himself. We are made in His likeness. And He understands our needs. Thank you Jesus.

My Prayers:

Lord God please help us as we read your word, help us in our understanding of you, help us to keep looking to you, help us to not give up in doing good. Lord show us the way, teach us I pray. Amen

Hebrews 13:1-3, 6-8, 15 & 20,21 Concluding Exhortations

Keep on loving each other as brothers. Do not forget to entertain strangers, for by doing so some people have entertained angels without knowing it. Remember those in prison as if you were their fellow prisoners, and those who are mistreated as if you yourselves were suffering.

V6: So we say with confidence, "The Lord is my helper; I will not be afraid. What can man do to me?"

Remember your leaders, who spoke the word of God to you. Consider their way of life and imitate their faith. Jesus Christ is the same yesterday and today and forever. Amen

V15: Through Jesus, therefore, let us continually offer to God a sacrifice of praise-- the fruit of the lips that confess his name. And do not forget to do good and to share with others, for with such sacrifices God is pleased.

V20: May the God of peace, who through the blood of the eternal covenant brought back from the dead our Lord Jesus, that great Shepard of the sheep, equip you with everything good for doing his will, and may he work in us what is pleasing to him, through Jesus Christ, to whom be the glory forever and ever. Amen

My prayers:

Lord God help me to remember what you have taught me and please give me peace, Help me to remember your suffering, so in mine; I will remember that you suffered more. I should be so grateful, Lord please give me a grateful heart. Teach us I pray Amen

---

James 1:26, 27 3:9-12 Listening and Doing

If anyone considers himself religious and yet does not keep a tight rein on his tongue, he deceives himself and his religion is worthless. Religion that God our Father accepts as pure and faultless is this: to look after orphans and widows in their distress and to keep oneself from being polluted by the world.

V3 With the tongue we praise our Lord and Father, and with it we curse men. Who have been made in Gods likeness. Out of the smane mouth comes praise and cursing. My brothers this should not be. Can both fresh water and salt water flow from the same spring? My brothers can a fig tree bear olives, or grapevine bear figs? Neither can salt spring produce fresh water.

V 7 All kinds of animals, birds, reptiles and creatures of the sea are been tamed by man, but no man can tame the tongue, it is restless evil, full of deadly poison.

This should not be!

This is very eye opening, message! One we should really take note of, and ask God to help us with. As we know God can tame the tongue, but only if we ask him and only put good stuff in our brain and keep asking God to help us, change us. I use to swear when I was younger, but I prayed God would change me and help me, He did, I don't swear as much, I have to say as much because sometimes I slip up and say a bad word, but I always ask God to forgive me and help me to not repeat it. I do have to say, the most I have said is the s word, but mostly I ask God to help me to think positive thoughts and to take away the bad thoughts. I know he can help you to, he has helped me and if you believe; He will help you to. We must trust Him who has our best interest at hand.

It has been hard living on my own again, it gets lonely and sometimes I just wish I had someone to talk to at night, I call friends but their busy with their own lives. It bothers me sometimes, and I try to remember they have their own struggles and cant help me, I find it hard. I want to do the right things and make the right decisions, so I turn to God and ask for guidance. I will remember the saying: Stinking Gremlins go away!

My Prayers:

Lord God please go before me today, show me the way, teach me and help me to help others, Lord you know my heart and you know how I feel, please give me courage to step out and make a difference in peoples lives, to go the distance, to not give up the fight. Please bring people in my life who can help me. And I will keep looking to you for guidance. Amen

---

James 5:7-12 Patience and Suffering

Be Patient, then, brothers, until the Lords coming. See how the farmer waits for the land to yield its valuable crop and how patient he is for the Autumn and spring rains. You to, be patient and stand firm, because the Lords coming is near. Dont grumble against each other, brothers, or you will be judged. The Judge is standing at the door!

Brothers as an example of patience in the face of suffering, take the prophets who spoke in the name of the Lord. As you know, we consider blessed those who have preserved. You have heard of Jobs preservice and have seen what the Lord finally brought about. The Lord is full of compassion and mercy. Above all, my brothers, do not swear- not by heaven or by earth or anything else. Let your "Yes" be yes, and your "No', no, or you will be condemned.

This is pretty important stuff, and should be thought about, prayed about and we should ask God to help us to be more patient. To be more engaged in relationships, to give more love.

I will give more of my love to all my family and friends. I will try to be more understanding and forgiving. I will ask God to help me and give me courage to keep going even when it gets tough.

Wisdom: That when I calmly look life in the eye, having grown wise from beating and flapping against its imperfections, learning to compromise, and accepting the fact that everyone and everything has its shortcomings. Life will have given me truth and taken in exchange, my youth. Auther Sara Teasdale

My Prayers:

Thank you Lord for granting me strength to live through the difficult times, and thank you for holding me up especially in my most vulnerable moments. Help me to have more courage in times of trouble, there is hope in you. Lord show me the way? Help me to be strong in adversity, and please take away all the bad thoughts Amen

---

Hebrew 2:1-4 Warning to Pay Attention.

We must pay more attention, therefore, to what we have heard so that we do not drift away. For if the message spoken by angels was binding, and every violation and disobedience received its just punishment, how shall we escape if we ignore such great salvation? This salvation, which was first announced by the Lord , was confirmed to us by those who heard him. God also testified to it by signs, wonders and various miracles, and gifts of the Holy Spirit distributed according to his will.

So its so important to keep the faith, keep reading his word and never stop praying, we must never give up hope, we must look to God for our everything. Our all! Seek, knock, and never give up the fight, we must keep looking to God for our needs. And asking the questions, He will reveal what He knows we need to know, In due time.

My Prayers:

Lord show us the way, teach us and help to us to understand your word, help us to not give up, help us to keep the faith, help us to keep looking to you for our guidance. You are our hope, our salvation. Lord I want to give you my all. May you shine your light through me to those that are lost and seeking. Amen

---

Daniel 12:1-4 The End Times

"At that time Michael, the great prince who protects your people, will rise. There will be a time of distress such has not happened from the beginning of nations until then. But at that time your people- and everyone who's name is written in the book-will be delivered. Multitudes who sleep in the dust of the earth will awake: Some to everlasting life, others to shame and everlasting contempt. Those who are wise will sine like the brightness of the heavens, and those who lead many to righteousness, like the stars for ever and ever. But you Daniel, close up and seal the words of the scroll until the time of the end. Many will go here and there to increase knowledge.

Daniel was a wise man, he was able to hear Gods voice and discern the right from the wrong, he was a person who had a close relationship with the Lord, God helped him understand and interpret dreams. God spoke to him; Daniel was a good man. He learned from his mistakes, and looked to the God of mercy for forgiveness and the Lord helped him. I think only a very few can do this, I wish I could here God more often and hear what He wants me to do. Like how do I publish these books and who can I trust.

My Prayers:

Lord show me the way, please bring the people in my life that can help me, I want to live your will and do the right things, Lord you know what I need before I ask, please Lord here my prayers, please send someone to help me. Amen

---

Psalm 16:1, 5, 9, 10 King David is talking.

Keep me safe, Oh God, for in you I take refuge.

Lord, you have assigned me my portion and my cup; you have made my lot secure. The boundary lines have fallen for me in pleasure places; surely I have a delightful inheritance.

Therefore my heart is glad and my tongue rejoices; my body will also rest secure, because you will not abandon me to the grave, nor will you let your Holy one see decay.

My Prayers:

Thank you Jesus for the great man David, he was a good man, he had his days, but he returned to you Oh God, you made him who he was. You spoke to him for us, to help us. Thank you Jesus; you are wonderful, please help me find a great job one that I will enjoy doing. Amen

---

Psalm 23

The Lord is my shepherd, I shall not be in want. He makes me lie down in green pastures, he leads me beside quiet waters, he restores my soul. He guides me in paths of righteousness for his name sake. Even though I walk through the valley of the shadow of death, I will fear no evil, for you are with me; your rod and your staff they comfort me. You prepare a table before me in the presence of my enemies. You anoint my head with oil; my cup overflows. Surely goodness and love will follow me all the days of my life, and I will dwell in the house of the Lord forever.

I love that one.

Its such a good one, it can help you in times of trouble and fear, please try and memorize it.

The Earth is His; he established it and everything in it, we must always remember that, God is supreme all knowing and all seeing. I believe God can change things for us, we first must believe. He knows are hearts and our minds, He even knows what we are going to do next. I believe God can change our situation and make it better. Trust Him.

My prayers:

Lord show me the way, help me I pray. I need a job to keep me going, Lord you know how much I need it, please provide. Thank you. Please forgive me of my sins, help me to be strong, and courageous and not give up. Amen

---

Nehemiah 9:6-10 The Israelites Confess Their Sins

"Blessed be your glorious name, may it be exalted above all blessing and praise. You alone are the Lord. You made the heavens, even the highest heavens, and all their sterry host, the earth and all that is on it, the sea and all that is in them. You give life to everything, and multitudes of heaven worship you. "You are the Lord God, who chose Abram and brought him out of Ur of the Chaldeans and named him Abraham. You found his heart faithful to you, and made a covenant with him to give his descendants the land of Canaanites, Hittites, Amorites, Perizzites, jebusites, and Girgashites. You have kept your promise because you are righteous. "You saw the suffering of our forefathers in Egypt; you heard their cry at the Red Sea. You sent miraculous signs and wonders against Pharaoh, against all his officials and all the people of his land, for you new how arrogantly the Egyptians treated them. You made a name for yourself, which remains till this day.

Wow, Abraham was very fortunate to have God put him in such a good position and to be a person who God himself trusted, to help him and his people. I pray the Lord can do the same for you and I, we can have our dreams, I hope God can give me a high paying Job and that I would really enjoy doing it. I pray the Lord can change my circumstances and make it right. And that one day I will be able to say Yes I am a writer, and I can make a difference in peoples lives. I can help people, this is why we are here, to help each other on our Journey, we can be successful in our lives. We can!

My Prayers:

Lord I am yours, do your will in me, help me to help the lost and give them a little bit of your love and direct them to you, through me, and help me be a good listener, help me to trust you with my all. Amen

---

Esther 2: 19-23 Mordecai Uncovers a Conspiracy

When the virgins were assembled a second time, Mordecai was sitting at the Kings gate. But Esther had kept secret her family background and nationality just as Madecai had told her to do, for she continued to follow Mordecai's instructions as she had done when he was brinning her up. During the time of Mordecai was sitting at the King's gate, Bigthana and Teresh, two of the kings officers who guarded the doorway, became angry and conspired to assassinate King Xeres. But Mordecai found out about the plot and told Queen Eshter, who in turn reported it to the king, giving credit to Mordecai. And when the report was investigated and found to be true, the two officials were hanged on a gallows. All this was reported in the book of annals in the presence of the king.

Esther was a good example of how we should be; Faithful.

She was faithful to her God and to her King.

My Prayers:

Thank you Lord for your good book, you are so wonderful, you knew in your great wisdom that we needed a book something to help us along life's journey, you knew we needed it before we did. In your great wisdom you who brought everything into existence and new how much we needed the love, you brought it here! You created the whole earth and everything in it, we should be so blessed to have you to, Thank you Lord God for all the blessings and peace you give. Please Lord help me in my time of needs, Amen

---

Psalm 9:1, 2, and 7-10, 13, 14 Psalm of Praise From David

I will praise you, O Lord, with all my heart; I will tell of all your wonders. I will be glad and rejoice in you; I will sing praises to your name, O Most High.

V7: The Lord reigns forever; he has a stablished his throne for judgment. He will judge the world in righteousness; he will govern the peoples with justice. The Lord is the refuge for the oppressed, in strong hold and times of trouble. Those who know your name will trust in you, for you Lord, have never forsaken those who seek you.**V13:** O Lord, see my enemies persecute me! Have mercy and lift me up from the gates of death, that I may declare your praises in the gates of the daughter Zion and in there rejoice in your salvation.

Yes the Psalm is a great place to go and find rest and some peace of mind, it helps me and gives me hope. I am also drawn to the Psalm because David is also my brothers name, and he has struggled for most of his life, he has a disability just like David in the bible, he had his struggles, as we all do, but his was how God made him and he did do so much for the Lord, He was made King after all! David was a strong man, just like my brother Dave, They are similar as they both have some struggles of mind, my brother cant read and write, something David had no problem with but he did struggle with other things; The David of the bible is a man of greatness, God had mercy on him and forgave him and then made him King, that is something. I believe God can do things like this still to this day, we must trust Him. We struggle and make things work out, but God is the one who we put our trust in and we look to him. When trouble comes, we should pray and trust.

My Prayers:

Lord help me trust you with everything. Thank you for watching over us and keeping us safe, we trust you and I give you my life, show me the way? And help me to be strong in times of trouble. Help me to not give up, Amen

---

Psalm 15:1-5 A Psalm of David

Lord, who may dwell in your sanctuary? Who may live on your holy hill? He whos walk is blameless and who does what is righteous, who speaks the truth from his heart and has no slander on his tongue, who does his neighbor no wrong and cast no slur on his fellowman, who despises those who fear the Lord, who keeps his oath even when it hurts, who lends his money without usury and does not except a bribe against the innocent. He who does those things will never be shaken.

I believe God can change our life around, we must trust him and keep following him, I have had a kinda hard life, I was abused as a child and it was hard. I talked about it in the first book. I had a hard time forgiving the men in my life, but I have and I feel better and more free, I find letting go is freeing and it helps you feel good inside, and it makes you want to help others, and give when we can. I know God wants us to give, I do when I can.

War-

Growing up is hard especially if you live in a country with wars, I am glad to be a Canadian and I am glad we are a free country and we help others around us. Yes we sent army to help the other country's but we haven't been in a war, per say. Thank God, I am grateful that we are not at war, I really feel for those people, I pray for those people. God sees what's happening, and it isn't going unnoticed. O Lord your hand saves me from such men. And I am free to go where i want, when I want and how I want. This is true freedom! And I am grateful. Today I will wait on the Lord.

My Prayers:

Thank you Lord God for your great mercy, for helping us, for loving us and for giving us. We have all things in this life that we need and more, we are blessed, I don't always feel blessed, but God says I am then I am. I will try and look to the bible to help me in my times of trouble. Lord you know what it is I need, please provide? Amen

---

Judges 6:7-17 Gideon

When the Israelite's cried to the Lord because of Mideon, he sent them a prophet, who said, "This is what the Lord, the God of Israel, says: I brought you up out of Egypt, out of the land of slavery. I snatched you from the power of Egypt and from the hand of all your oppressors. I drove them from before you and gave their land. I said to you, "I am the Lord your God; do not worship the gods of Amorities, in whose land you live'. But you have not listen to me". The angel of the Lord came and sat down under the oak in Ophrah that belong to Joash the Abiezrite, where his son was threshing wheat in a winepress to keep it from the Midianites. When the angel of the Lord appeared to Gideon, he said, "The Lord is with you, mighty warrior." " But sir," Gideon replied, "if the Lord is with us, why has all this happen to us? Where are all his wonders that our fathers told us about when they said, 'Did not the Lord bring us up out of Egypt?" But now the Lord has abandoned us and put us into the hand of Midian."

" The Lord turned to him and said, "Go in the strength you have and save Israel out of Midian's hand. Am I not sending you?" "But Lord, Gideon asked, "How can I save Israel? My clan is the weakest in Manasseh, and I am least in my family." The Lord answered, "I will be with you, and you will strick down all the Midianties together." Gideon replied, "If now I have found favor in your eyes, give me a sign that it is really you talking to me. Pease do not go away till I come back and bring my offering and set it before you." And the Lord said "I will wait until you return."

Wow, that is something. He said he would wait. And that he would give them strength to go and fight, I believe if we ask He will answer, we must first ask for forgiveness and with a pure heart he will answer.

My Prayers:

Lord you know my heart, please forgive me of my sins, and turn my life around, help me find work and find a place to give my talents, to help the lost and to feel again. I want to do the right things and make the right decisions, help me with this I pray, Amen

Sometimes we go down the wrong path and feel lost, if we trust Jesus and ask for guidance He will provide. He will here our cries for help. He will come. And He will help us in our time of trouble.

Judges 8:23-28 Gideon's Ephod

The Israelites said to Gideon, "Rule over us-you, your son and your grandson- because you have saved us out of the hand of Midian." But Gideon told them, "I will not rule over you, nor will my son rule over you. The Lord will rule over you." And he said, "I do have one request, that each of you give me an earing from your share of the plunder." (It was the custom of the Ishmaelites to wear gold, earrings.) They answered, "We'll be glad to give them," So they spread out a garment, and each man threw a ring from his plunder onto it. The weight of the gold rings he asked for came to seventeen hundred shekels, not counting the ornaments, the pendants and the purple garments worn by the kings of Midian or the chains that were on their camels necks. Gideon made the gold into an ephod, which he placed in Ophrah, his town. All Israel prostituted themselves by worshiping it there, and it became a snare to Gideon and his family. Thus Midian was subdued before the Israelites and did not raise its head again. During Gideon's lifetime, the land enjoyed peace for forty years.

Gideon's son of Joash died at a good old age and was buried in the tomb of his father Joash in Ophrah of the Abiezrites.

When I awoke this morning, I was thinking about work again, wish I could get these books published and start writing the kids books. Its taking me a long time, and I hope I can sell them. I know people have said I could and said I should keep on writing, even if I haven't published one yet. So here I am writing still. And Hoping one day I can publish them, for now I keep writing.

My prayers:

Lord you know me and how I feel, Lord help me, encourage me and uplift me, I need you and I need to know this is what you want me to do? I need to know I can make it as a writer, and not give up. I may not know how to publish but one day I am hoping someone comes along who can help me. And just maybe make a good friend, Lord willing. Lord, please give me insight. Amen

---

Samuel 8:1-12 Israel Asks for a King

When Samuel grew old, he appointed his sons as judges for Israel. The names of his firstborn was Joel and the name of his second one was Abijah, and they served in Beersheba. But his sons did not walk in his ways. They turned aside after dishonest gain and accepted bribes and perverted justice. So all the elders of Israel gathered together and came to Samuel at Ramah. They said to him, "You are old, and your sons do not walk in your ways; now appoint a king to lead us, such as all the other nations have." But when they said, "Give us a king to lead us," this displeased Samuel, so he prayed to the Lord. And the Lord told him: "Liston to all that the people are saying to you; it is not you they have rejected, but they have rejected me as there King. As they have done from the day I brought them up out of Egypt until this day, forsaking me and serving other gods, so they are doing to you. Now listen to them; but warn them solemnly and let them know what the King who will reign over them will do. Samuel told all the people who were asking him for a king. He said, "This is what the king who will reign over you will do: He will take your sons and make the serve with his chariots and horses, and they will run in front of his chariots. Some he will assign to be commanders of thousands and of fifties, and others to plow his ground and reap his harvest, and still others make weapons of war and equipment for his chariots.

That was a long one today, I see it took a long time for them to find a good king, and his men all did not stay faithful, some left the towns. But the ones who stayed he helped them.

I feel it is hard sometimes, especially when God takes time to answer a prayer request, I often wonder about that, why does it take sometimes a long time to answer the prayer? And other times he answers right away. I guess we wont know the mystery until we get to heaven. And all our prayers answered and all our questions answered. It will be a glorious day!

My Prayers:

Lord help me make the right decisions today, help me and guide me. Show me the way and teach me I pray. Lord please here my prayers. Amen

---

1 Samuel 12:1-8 Samuel's Farewell speech

You can read the first chapters up until chapter 5, I am going to write from there; Samuel was talking to the people.

V5: Samuel said to them, "The Lord has witness against you, and also his anointed is witness this day that you have not found anything in my hand." "He is a witness," they said. Then Samuel said to the people, "It is the Lord who appointed Moses and Aaron and brought your forefathers up out of Egypt. Now then, stand here, because I am going to confront you with evidence before the Lord as to all righteous acts performed by the Lord for you and your fathers. After Jacob entered Egypt, they cried to the Lord for help, and the Lord sent Moses and Aaron, who brought your forefathers out of Egypt and settled them in this place.

So it is important to listen to our God and be good and help others when we can, We are children of God and should do good. Just as the Lord said do good to others, help the lonely and the lost, show them mercy, when we can we help. Gods book has so much to learn from; if we keep reading and looking to him who loves us unconditionally, we can go on.

My prayers:

Lord you know my heart and you have made me, please go before me and make a way, help me I pray. Lord I need you now and forever more, come and help me I pray. Lord please be with all who are reading this and who need you. Lord show us the way? God oh how I need you, come and help me I pray. Amen

---

Samuel 13:1-7 Samuel Rebukes Saul

Saul was thirty years old when he became king, and he reigned over Israel forty two years. Saul chose three thousand men from Israel; two thousand were with him at Micmash and in the hill country of Bethel, and a thousand were with Johnathan at Gibeah in Benjamin. The rest of the men he sent back to their homes. Johnathan attacked the Philistine out post at Geba, and the Philistines heard about it. Then Saul had the trumpet blown throughout the land and said, "Let the Hebrews hear!" So all Israel heard the news: "Saul has attacked the Philistines outpost, and now Israel has become a stench to the Philistines." And the people were summoned to join Saul at Gilgal. The Philistines assembled to fight Israel, with three thousand chariots, six thousand charioteers, and soldiers as numerous as the sand on the seashore. They went up and camped at Micmash, east of Beth Aven. When the men of Israel saw that their situation as critical and that their army was hard pressed, they hid in caves and thickets, among the rocks, and pits in the criterns. Some Hebrews even crossed the Jordan to the land of Gad and Gilead.

Their is a lot in the bible to read, and it has a lot of wars, it seems. I don't like wars, most people don't, I think we should all help each other, that's what the Lord God wants us to do, so why all these wars? Why must people be so greedy? I know we all need money and things, but we don't need to go to war over it. I am glad I am Canadian, I know I have said it before, but I am glad. And proud to say I am Canadian. I want peace and I think most people do; Lord help us have peace.

My Prayers:

Lord please give us peace today, show me the way teach me I pray; Help me to help others as much as I can, with what you give me. Lord please help me to use my money wisely and to do good with it, as you provide. Lord help me to show mercy and be kind to all. Forgive me and help me to be strong. Lord please go before me and make a way. Amen

---

2 Samuel 22:1-4 David's Song of Praise

David sang to the Lord the words of this song when the Lord delivered him from the land of all his enemies and from the hand of Saul. H said: "The Lord is my rock, my fortress and my deliverer; my God is my rock, in whom I take refuge, my shield and the horn of my salvation. He is my strong hold, my refuge and my savior-from violent men you save me. I call to the Lord who is worthy of praise, and I am saved from my enemies.

What a great way to say thank you and to be grateful, then to sing praises to our God, he loves to here us sing, even if we're not that good, I think I can sing good. I was in choir and have enjoyed singing in Church, and I love to sing praises to my Lord, He is good, and helps us in our time of need.

My Prayers:

Lord show me who I can help today, help me to make the right decisions and do the right things; help me discern right from wrong. I pray I can make enough money to pay my bills and have some spending money to. Lord please here my prayers. I need you Lord. Amen

---

1 Chronicles 11:4-9 David Conquers Jerusalem

David and all the Israelites marched to Jerusalem (That is Jebus). The Jebusites who lived there said to David, "You will not get in here." Nevertheless, David captured the fortress of Zion, the city of David. David had said, "who ever leads the attack on the Jebusites will become commander in chief." Joab son of Zeruiah went up first, and so he received the command. David then took up residence in the fortress, and so it was called the city of David. He build up the city around it, from the supporting terraces to the surrounding wall, while Joab restored the rest of the city. And David became more and more powerful, because the Lord Almighty was with him.

David was a good king, he had his faults we all do, but he did make a good king after all.

My prayers:

Lord please here my prayers, I need money to pay my bills and I don't know where it will come from, please help me. Amen

---

1 Chronicles 13:1-8 Brining Back the Ark

David conferred with each of his officers, the commanders of thousands and commanders of hundreds. He then said to the whole assembly of Israel, "If it seems good to you and if it is the will of the Lord our God, let us send word far and wide to the rest of our brothers throughout the territories of Israel, and also to the priests and Levites who are with them in their towns and pasture lands, to come and join us, for we did not inquire of it during the reign of Saul." The whole assembly agreed to do this, because it seemed right to all the people. So David assembled all the Israelites, from the Shihor River in Egypt to Lebo Hamath, to bring the Ark of God from Kiriath Jearim. David and all the Israelites with him went to Baalah of Judah (Kiriath Jearim) to bring up from there the Ark of God the Lord, who is enthroned between the cherubim- the Ark that is called by the Name. They moved the Ark of God from Abinadabs house on a new cart with Uzzah and Ahio guiding it. David and all the Israelites were celebrating with all their might before God, with song and with harps, lyres, tambourines, cymbals and trumpets.

They were happy to celebrate for they had done a good thing, they had brought the Ark back. And were very happy with it. David was happy that day, and all his men. They must of felt wow we did it, we accomplished something of great value to them, and they were celebrating that they brought it back.

I would be happy to, knowing I am protected and saved. And that God was in our presence. That we could have him close to our homes. But we do! We have the Holy Spirit and he lives within us, so we do have God with us always. Even if we don't feel it, he is with us.

My Prayers:

Lord thank you for helping us, for answered prayers and for always being there for us, for knowing what we need before we ask, thank you. Please help me today. Amen

---

1 Chronicles 15:1-4 The Ark Brought to Jerusalem

After David had constructed buildings for himself in the city of David, he prepared a place for the Ark of God and pitched a tent for it. Then David said, "No one but the Levites may carry the Ark of God, because the Lord chose them to carry the Ark of the Lord and to minister before him forever." David assembled all Israel in Jerusalem to bring up the Ark of the Lord to the place he had prepared for it. He called together the descendants of Aaron and the Levites.

You can go on to read the clans and then continue to read the accounts of David. It is very interesting. And I found out more about David. He was a great King. Someone who look to God through out his life, he struggled just like us, he was know different in that matter, and he was human, so he did make mistakes, we all. But he was a man after Gods heart. He ruled for forty years; Seven in Hebron and thirty three in Jerusalem and died a good old age.

God was with him and he was a successful king. I believe if we trust God and give him our life He will help us, he will give us what we need.

My Prayers:

Lord thank you for giving us our needs, thank you for keeping us safe, I do need you Lord God, please help me, you know what I need before I ask, show me the way o Lord. Amen

---

1 Chronicles 16:1-6 The Ark of God

They brought the Ark of God and set it inside the tent that David had pitched for it, and they presented burnt offerings and fellowship offerings before God. After David had finished sacrificing the burnt offerings and fellowship offerings, he blessed the people in the name of the Lord. Then he gave a loaf of bread, a cake of dates and a cake of raisins to each Israelite man and woman. He appointed some of the Levites to minister before the Ark of the Lord, to make petition, to give thanks, and to praise the Lord, the God of Israel: Asaph was the chief, Zechariah second, then Jeiel, Shemiramoth,Jehiel, Mattihiah, Eliab, Benaiah, Obed-Edom and Jeiel. They were to play the lyes and harps,Asaph was to sound the cymbals, and Benaiah and Jahaziel the priests were to blow the trumpets regularly before the Ark of the covenant of God.

There is so much going on there, and more to discover, and the more we read the bible the more we learn, I have read most of it, I find some of the books of the bible are hard to read, it takes great wisdom to understand, and maybe one day I can. I will keep asking God to lead me and help me understand. This book has a lot of insight on the old testaments lately, I must keep reading, Lord help me understand. There is always hope.

My Prayers:

Lord please help us understand your word, you gave it to us so we can know you more, and have a relationship with you, please help me understand it. Help me to keep looking to you for guidance and for hope. Amen

We read in Matthew this day.

Chronicles 17:1-15 Gods Promise to David

Matthew 1 The Genealogy of Jesus.

Chor: 17:1-15 Gods promise to David

After David was settled into his palace, he said to Nathan the prophet, "Here I am, living in a palace of Cedar, while the Ark of the covenant of the Lord is under a tent". Nathan replied to David, "Whatever you have in mind, do it, for God is with you." That night the word of God came to Nathan, saying.:

"Go and tell my servant David. 'this is what the Lord says: You are not the one to build me a house to dwell in. I have not dwelt in a house from the day I brought Israel up out of Egypt to this day. I have moved from one tent site to another from one dwelling place to another. Wherever I have moved with all the Israelites, did I ever say to any of their leaders whom I commanded to shepherd my people, Why have you not built me a house of cedar?" "Now then tell my servant David, "This is what the Lord Almighty says: I took you from the pasture and from the following flock, to be ruler over my people Israel. I have been with you wherever you have gone, and I have cut off all your enemies from before you. Now I will make your name like the names of the greatest men of the earth. And I will provide a place for my people Israel and will plant them so that they can have a home of their own and no longer to be disturbed. Wicked people will not oppress them anymore, as they did at the beginning and have done ever since the time I appointed leaders over my people Israel. I will also subdue all your enemies. "I declare to you that the Lord will build a house for you: When your days are over and you go to be with your fathers, I will raise up your offspring to succeed you, one of your own sons, and I will establish his Kingdom. He is the one who will build a house for me, and I will establish his throne forever. I will be his father, and he will be my son, I will never take my love away from him, as I took it away from your predecessor. I will set him over my house and my Kingdom forever. His throne will be established forever." Nathan reported to David all the words of his entire revelation.

Matthew 1:1

A record of the genealogy of Jesus Christ the son of David, the son of Abraham. Please read it. It will help you understand. Thank you

Wow what a dream, can you imagine? Maybe for some this happens but for most of us we don't get revelations. God can give them to anybody. God can do all things.

My Prayers:

Lord show us the way, speak to us in your loving ways and teach us how to live. How to be kind for those who don't know how, teach us the way. We want to be good servants help us in this task. Amen

Have you ever felt like know one really understands you? That you are alone, and wonder if you will ever get your dreams? That's where I am at right now, lonely and I have good reason to be lonely, no real friends and no family close by, other then my kids. I lean on them a lot, maybe more then I should; but there my kids, and I believe God gave them to me. But I am very lonely today, and I woke up feeling this way, and I started to think of my past and how I have struggled with this loneliness most of my life; I never will understand why my friends never call, or visit. They have their own lives, but if there my friends why don't they call or visit? When I had kids; that's when I lost all my friends, they stop hanging out with me, it was so hard. I miss those old friends, I wish they would call me. Know one ever calls me. Why, what have I done so bad that I don't get friends calling. Its so frustrating and it makes me so sad, I a m a good person, if I ever hurt you I would say sorry, I would tell you how much I am sorry for hurting you. I have always been that way, my whole life. So why don't I have all those friends around me? Why doesn't anyone call me, do they care do they even think of me. Probably not. They never call or write or anything, so they probably never think of me. I am their past. I hate being alone. I am and will be for some time until I get better, If I ever will I don't know. Its up to God to heal my mind. Lord please heal me, please heal my broken heart. Its so hard going it alone, being single has always been hard for me, I was a needy child growing up, and maybe that has been my down fall, I have struggled all my life. And Now I find myself alone again and doing it on my own, which I chose to do, because I didn't want to be in an abusive relationship any more. I been hurt to many times. And Now I am having a hard time again; I wish God could bring some good friends in my life, I pray for friends. Lord please bring the right people in my life to help me with my books, Please Lord I need your help, I don't have the money or the knowledge to publish or knowhow, so Lord you know my situation and you know how I feel, please bring them in my life, I need a partner who understands me completely and who can support me in my dreams. Amen

When you are growing up, and you have friends who say their your friends, but never call you or write or visit, you have to wonder are they truly your friends? I lost all my friends when I started my family, they just didn't hang out with me or call anymore, they just stopped being there for me.

It was so hard loosing them. I guess they weren't true friends. I miss a lot of them, they have their own lives now. They probably never think of me, oh well. I will just have to keep chunking alone and do my part here on earth. I cant wait to get to heaven. I will have no more loneliness and pain in my heart. Lord please come soon. Amen

Loneliness:

I found this in my bible, the Author is Millie Stamm

A Prison Experience

Joseph attained a place of prominence in Egypt by a difficult road of loneliness and injustice. His brothers, hated him in tensely, sold him into slavery, and he was taken to Egypt, separated from family and friends, he must fo been lonely and homesick. But "The lord was with Joseph." Through a series of events over which he had no control, he was imprisoned. Joseph's imprisonment was a training period for God's future plans for him. He learned patience while in prison. Authority given him over the prisoners developed his leadership ability. This was preparation for him later when he directed food distribution during a severe famine. Joseph may have questioned why his brother mistreated him; why he was sold into slavery; why he was imprisoned on a charge which he was innocent. Yet he didn't let his prison experience embitter him. Although he didn't understand it, nor could he see what the future held, he was aware of God's presence with him in prison. Today you maybe in prison, Perhaps you are misunderstood by family, or you maybe far away from home, and lonely, whatever your prison experience, humanly speaking, there maybe know way out, no immediate solution. What is your reaction? Are you rebellious? Are you questioning God? God knows the lessons we need to learn, lessons of patience, submission and self-denial. Our faith may need strengthening. We may be so concerned that God removes us from prison, that we miss the lessons he has for us in prison. Our prison term may seem long, but the God who was with Joseph when he was taken into Egypt, and the God who was with him when he was put in prison, is the God who is with us today.

My Prayers:

Thank you lord for my bible, I am so grateful to have such a good book in my home, it has helped me so much. I am also glad I picked it up. Thank you Lord. Amen

I woke up this am not feeling to good, in my tummy. I have a bit of a cold and I am not feeling to hot, but I am still going to church this am, as it is my duty to give my God all that I can. I don't have money to give but I am still going because that's where He wants me. I need to go because it helps me. I usually feel better after the service.

I pray the Lord will heal me and help me feel better. I am going to be finishing up with this book and starting my kids books. So I hope you have learned a lot and have grown in your spiritual life, continue down that path, don't turn left or right, just keep looking to the Lord for all your needs, he will provide. Just remember it is on His time not ours; so be patient, as the Lord works differently then we do. His timing is great. May God Bless you in your faith Journey.

My Prayers:

Dear God; please be with each and everyone who has picked up my book to read, please help them find what they are looking for, may you give them peace within. Amen

---

2 Chronicles 7:1-12 6:18 The dedication of The Temple

Please read through them.

Receiving His Blessing

This article is written from Hannah Whitall Smith

To some the promise of the Father comes as a mighty and overwhelming power; to others he comes as the tender and gentle presence of love. But either way He always makes his presence manifest; and at that day, whenever it comes, the word of our Lord, which he spoke to his disciples concerning this wondrous gift, are invariably fulfilled. "On that day you will realize that I am in my Father, and you are in me, and I am in you" (John 14:20). We may have believed it before because God says it is so in the Scriptures, but from the moment we receive it we know it by the testimony of an inward consciousness that is unassailable by any form of questioning or doubt. The Israelites believed the Lord was in their midst all along in their wonderings and in their years of bondage. But when the Temple was built, they all saw how "Fire came down from heaven...and the glory of the Lord filled the temple" (2 Chronicles 7:1), they new it. We cannot wonder that at once, without the need of any command from Solomon, they bowed themselves with their faces to the ground and worshiped and praised the Lord. Words fail in seeking to tell of the blessedness of this inner life of divine union, and the spirit stand amazed before such glorious possibilities of experience! With Solomon we explain , "but will God really dwell on earth with men? The heavens even the highest heavens, cannot contain you. How much less this temple I have built!" And the Lord answered, as he did to Solomon, "I have heard your prayer and have chosen this place for myself". Amen

That is a wonderful passage, I think we all need to trust a little more, love a little more and give a little more. Peace be with you all. As you go on with your journey and walk with the Lord, please give time to receive and give, for when we give it pleases the Lord and when we give, it gives hope to the one who receives it.

My prayers:

Lord you know out hearts, please heal us, forgive us and help us to be good and faithful servants. Amen

Becoming a Christian is not always easy, it will take giving up your will power and letting God in, and letting Him do the work He has planned to do; we must trust first and know deep within ourselves that this is true genius faith. And that you desire a deep relationship with the Lord, He knows how you feel and He knows your sufferings; if you have already excepted Him great, but for those who are still on the fence, please don't hesitate any longer, you will feel the love enter and the hope renewed, so don't let things be a stumbling block.

God is in control after all weather you believe or not He believes in you. And wants you to believe in yourself and his power to delivery you from the bonds. What ever it maybe that your not sure about, its in the bible. God loves all, he doesn't have favorites

He Loves you and wants what's best for you. He can give you the peace you have been so longing for.

Life has many twists and turns and we never know what will happen so don't give it another day. Trust Him who has your best interest at heart. Remember Jesus walked this life too and knows your suffering personally. He understands, He loves you more then you know.

Mark 14: 1-9 Jesus Anointed at Bethany

Now the Passover and the Feast of Unleavened Bread were only two days away, and the chief priests and the teachers of the law were looking for some sly way to arrest Jesus and kill him. But not during the feast," they said, "or the people may riot". While he was in Bethany, recling at the table in the home of a man known as Simon the leper, a woman came with an alabaster jar of very expensive perfume, made of pure nard. She broke the jar and poured the perfume on his head. Some of those prence were saying indignantly to one another, "Why this waste of perfume? It could of been sold for more then a years wages and the money given to the poor. "And the rebuked her harshly. "Leave her alone," said Jesus. "why are you bothering her? She has done a beautiful thing to me. The poor you will always have with you, and you can help them anytime you want. But you will not always have me. She did what she could. She poured perfume on my body beforehand to prepare for my burial. I tell you the truth, wherever the gospel is preached throughout the world, what she has done will also be told, in memory of her.

What a powerful statement. I believe Jesus was trying to prove to them, that they need to just trust and believe, as this woman has done. We don't have Jesus here in person any more but we have the Holy Spirit which is in us and helps us to do the right things, if we just take time to here Him speak.

It has to be some place quit as the Holy spirit speaks, with all the noise in this life, we often don't take the time to here him. He will speak and dose; you just need to be alone with him and listen. Take the time to listen. The world is a crazy place and very evil. We must take the time to be still and listen. I can say it maybe hard for some, it was for me at first. I didn't realize how Jesus was trying to talk to me, and I didn't take the timeout to just be still, and listen. We must for Him who loves us so much more then we realize. Jesus walked this earth, and He understands you, He can give you rest.

My Prayers: Let's pray

Lord show us your way, teach us I pray. For we get lost in all the stuff, and we need you. Lord help me to help others. Lord you know my heart and what is happening to me right now, Lord I give you my life and I want to walk with you for the rest of my life, show me the way, teach me I pray and help me with my decisions, help me to make the right decisions. Lord please give us peace and help us to help others. For you know me completely. I love you Lord God Amen

---

Ecclesiastes 3:1-8 A Time for Everything

There is a time for everything, a season for every activity under heaven.

A time to be born, and a time to die, a time to plant and a time to uproot, a time to kill and a time to heal, a time to tear down and a time to build, a time to weep and a time to laugh, a time to mourn and a time to dance, a time to scatter stones and a time to gather them, a time to embrace and a time to refrain, a time to search and a time to give up, a time to keep and a time to throw away, a time to tear and a time to mend, a time to be silent and a time to speak, a time to love and a time to hate, a time for war and a time for peace.

There are so many things in this life that will try to bring us down, we must keep looking to the Lord and asking for hope and peace within this fallen world we live in. We must keep bringing love and happiness where ever we go. Smile more, laugh often and be open to learning new things, as life can bring you down, learn to help others, learn a new song, teach someone something new. We must keep teaching and learning.

May God bless you as you do. Amen

Rejoice:

There should be a lot of laughter and games in the family. I don't know of anything better to relieve the inevitable tension that comes when people live under the same roof. A teenager who was having trouble with his parents (Good friends of ours) told them one day at the table, "If we couldn't all laugh together around this table, I wouldn't be able to stand this family." Love and laughter hold us together.

By: Ingrid Trobisch

My Prayers:

Dear Lord please give u peace today, as we go about our business help us to smile more, laugh often and give more, help us to help others and never stop loving. Lord you know our hearts, show us the way and keep us I pray. Amen

"We need something called self-denial (Not denying the self, but denying the self to indulge in wrongdoing). To think and pray about: Choose the good and live. Be long on self-denial in others ways, too.

Yes we must look to God and try our best to not sin, if we do we must repent and ask God to forgive us, and then turn from the sin. We must because then we will feel better, and we will make the right decisions. If we seek God first and give him our all we will be conquerors in all that we do. Amen

Seek out the good in all, give more hugs, tell someone their special, give that smile to all. And you will feel better.

May all your wishes come true and your dreams be many.

If you are a Christian single who is preoccupied with getting married to the point that you are frustrated day in and day out, week in and week out, then you are living outside the will of God. 1 Corinthians 7:28 You can say I want to be free from this burden, and God will help you focus more on him. And He will give you something that is more important like serving Him, and doing his will. Don't let other people distract you from your calling, when God reveals to you what your calling is, do it. Don't delay, just follow him and He will direct your path, He will guide you and protect you. Being successful as a single is so important to u you and Him, he wants to see you successful and making money for yourself. If you are not able to work, volunteering is a great way to give back and it makes you feel so good inside. It gives you meaning in life. And when we help others they are happy and that makes us happy, then we're all benefiting from it. The world is a lot better when we give back to it. God will provide all your needs, and then some. Trust him and give him your all.

My Prayers:

Lord show us how to treat others, help us in our time of need and give us hope for the future. Lord you have our hearts, and I am living for you Lord, help me to be kind and loving even to the evil person, as you have said, Love your enemies and be kind. Thank you Jesus for keeping us safe. Amen

Psalm 6:8

Away from me, all you who do evil, for the Lord has heard my weeping. The Lord has heard my cry for mercy; the Lord accepts my prayer. All my enemies will be ashamed and dismayed; they will turn back in sudden disgrace.

The Lord does hear our cry's for help, he will deliver you from your pain, trust him he is working in the back round, and he know your pain. He will come through for you, be patient and wait on the Lord, sometimes we have long suffering and we don't know why, if we look back on our days we may see our sin, God has been there from the beginning and will be there till the end, so don't give up hope, he will deliver you. Say this prayer: O Lord my God, I take refuge in you, save and deliver me from all who pursue me. I trust you with my life, please deliver me Amen. God heard your cry for help, trust him.

My Prayer:

O Lord please help us in our distrust, give us hope show us the way to go, teach us your ways, and help us I pray, Lord you know our hearts, you know us completely, teach us to number our days and give you our all. Help us in our weakness and give us hope. Amen

---

Psalm 4:4-8

In your anger do not sin, when you are on your beds, search your hearts and be silent. Offer right sacrifices and trust in the Lord. Many are asking, "Who can show us any good?" let the light of your face shine upon us, O Lord. You have filled my heart with greater joy then when their grain and new wine abound. I will lie down and sleep in peace, for you alone, O Lord, make me dwell in safety. Amen!

This is a great prayer, David was a great King, yes he did wrong, but don't we all fall in our lives, he was no different, he had his issues to, and we must not judge, as God says do not judge, Least we be judged. God chose David, and he new what he was doing, God new what mistakes he would make before hand and he still chose him, God is good. David made a lot of songs and I guess that's why there is a book of Psalms, he expressed his feeling and made music doing so. David was a great king, and he made a lot of sacrifices, David was a man of justice, he helped build a nation, and had many kids. Yes he made some bad choses, don't we all. I need to stop looking at other people's issues and face our own. We need to ask God for guidance and look to the saints. Amen

My Prayers:

Lord thank you for all the support you have given me over the years, thank you for trusting me in doing your work here on earth, Thank you for trusting me in this mission. Please help me and direct me on my path, show me where to go and with whom. I shall lift up on wings and fly, and I will be with you and you with me. Amen

I realize that life is not just about getting things, but more about giving things, your time, your hands, your heart, and giving to help the lost to help the child, to help the elderly. We are who we are and I will be the best that I can be... Amen

Credits...

Alma my grandma she believed in me when I felt know one else did. Thank you God for sending your one and only son, so we can be saved. Thank you for talking to me and guiding me. You truly are 3 in one... Thank you to my 2 beautiful daughters, Roxanne and Crystal.

CPSIA information can be obtained
at www.ICGtesting.com
Printed in the USA
LVHW022258240522
719535LV00015B/488